J. J. Strause

Prof Phil/Chr Doct

Lincoln Chr. Seminary

1968

The Modern Tongues Movement

Robert Glenn Gromacki

The Modern Tongues

Movement

Robert Glenn Gromacki, Th. D.

Presbyterian and Reformed Publishing Company
Philadelphia, Pennsylvania
1967

Distributed By
BAKER BOOK HOUSE
Grand Rapids, Mich.

TO
MY WIFE

faithful companion
and
loving mother
this volume is affectionately dedicated

ACKNOWLEDGMENTS

The author desires to express sincere gratitude to Dr. Herman A. Hoyt, Dr. Homer A. Kent, Jr., and Dr. John C. Whitcomb, Jr., for their constructive suggestions. Special thanks must be given to the administration of Cedarville College, who granted a leave of absence and financial help so that this book might be written.

The author also wishes to express public thanks to his wife, who spent many hours typing and re-typing the several drafts of the manuscript. He is also indebted to the wise counsel and direction of Mr. Charles H. Craig, director of the Presbyterian and Reformed Publishing Company, in the final preparation of this work.

Last but certainly not least, praise belongs to our God who has provided salvation through His Son, Jesus Christ (John 3:16) and sanctification through His Word (John 17:17). May this volume be used to bring honor and glory to Him.

ROBERT G. GROMACKI
Chairman, Division of Biblical Education
Cedarville College
Cedarville, Ohio

CONTENTS

CHAPTER I

INTRODUCTION

Practically every generation of Christendom has witnessed the development of some new movement (good or bad) within its ranks. The apostles had to guard the truth against the Judaizers and the rise of incipient Gnosticism. The post-apostolic era was full of controversy and of the development of new isms—Docetism, Cerinthianism, Eutychianism, Nestorianism, Sabellianism, Arianism, etc. Augustine struggled with Pelagianism. Even the period of the Dark Ages saw the activity of the ana-Baptists and the institution of the various Roman Catholic orders (Augustinian, Dominican, Franciscan, Jesuits, etc.). The Sixteenth Century gave birth to the mighty Protestant Reformation with its subsequent developments of the major church groups (Lutheran, Reformed, Anglican, Presbyterian) and the minor dissenters (Baptists, Methodists, etc.). Later, American Christendom contributed many distinctive groups— Mormons, Campbellites, Jehovah's Witnesses, Seventh Day Adventists, etc. The Twentieth Century has also witnessed its share of new developments. One key movement has been Pentecostalism with its emphasis upon the Holy Spirit and spiritual gifts. American Protestantism, itself, became divided into liberal and fundamental groups which resulted in the formation of new denominations. The old liberalism soon gave way to the rise of neo-orthodoxy and neo-liberalism. It has also promoted the ecumenical movement with its ultimate goal, the merger with the Roman Catholic Church. Even conservative Protestantism has not remained stagnant. Today, it is divided into fundamentalism and the new evangelicalism. Now, the newest movement to the American Christian scene is the Charismatic revival or the new Pentecostalism with its special emphasis upon healing and speaking in tongues. Less than ten years old, it has made a profound impact upon the church life of all denominations. Since this is a contemporary movement, it behooves each Christian to become acquainted with its basic nature and to examine it in the light of Scripture.

Importance of the Study

The very fact that the phenomenon of speaking in tongues or glossolalia (from the Greek *glossa*, tongue, and *laleo*, to speak) is found in the Bible should be cause enough for a thorough investigation. The phenomenon is mentioned in three books (Mark, Acts, I Corinthians). As a significant part of early church life, it is always related to the ministry of the Holy Spirit. It was the evidence of the Spirit's descent on the day of Pentecost (Acts 2:1-4) and of the initial reception of the Spirit in at least two cases (Acts 10:44-48; 19:1-7). Speaking in tongues was also a spiritual gift being exercised by the Corinthian church (I Cor. 12-14). An understanding of the nature and purposes of such phenomena in Biblical times is therefore imperative for each believer.

The rapid growth of Pentecostalism in the twentieth century also contributes to the importance of this study. *Time* called it the "fastest growing church in the hemisphere."[1] *Life* regarded it as "the third force," equal in significance to Roman Catholicism and historic Protestantism.[2] Henry P. Van Dusen, past president of Union Theological Seminary (New York), felt that the Pentecostal movement with its emphasis upon the Holy Spirit was "a revolution comparable in importance with the establishment of the original Apostolic Church and with the Protestant Reformation."[3] Such declarations take on even more significance when one realizes that speaking in tongues is the "most distinctive doctrine and perhaps the most spectacular feature of the Pentecostal Movement."[4] This important segment of American Protestantism cannot be ignored; contrariwise, it should be understood completely.

Less than twenty years ago, Brumback confessed: "We might as well face the facts: speaking in tongues is not acceptable anywhere except in the Pentecostal Movement."[5] This statement could not be made today, because speaking in tongues is *now* being accepted as a part of normal personal and church life among Baptists, Episcopalians, Lutherans, Methodists, Presbyterians, and

---

[1] "Fastest-Growing Church in the Hemisphere," *Time*, LXXX (November 2, 1962), p. 56.
[2] "The Third Force in Christendom," *Life*, XLIV (June 9, 1958), p. 113.
[3] Cited by John L. Sherrill,. *They Speak With Other Tongues* (New York: McGraw-Hill Book Company, 1964), p. 27.
[4] Carl Brumback, *What Meaneth This?* (Springfield, Mo.: The Gospel Publishing House, 1947), pp. 99, 147.
[5] *Ibid.*, pp. 175-76.

even Catholics. This outburst of tongues among the historic denominations has been called the New Penetration, the New Pentecostalism, Charismatic Renewal (or Revival), and the modern tongues movement. Both liberal and conservative churches, schools, mission boards, and publications have felt the impact of this new movement. It has been so widespread that even secular communications (radio, television, newspaper, magazines) have given attention to it. Thus, it becomes important for every believer to understand this new manifestation of tongue-speaking.

Research for this work has centered in personal Bible study, in standard theologies and commentaries, and in contemporary publications (magazines and journals). Books dealing with this contemporary phenomenon are rare. All English Scriptural quotations are taken from the Authorized Version, and all Greek words are taken from *Nestle's Greek New Testament* (*Novum Testamentum Graece*).

CHAPTER II

A HISTORICAL SURVEY OF SPEAKING IN TONGUES

In order to understand the contemporary tongues movement fully, a working knowledge of the history of the phenomenon is imperative. Advocates of glossolalia claim that the phenomenon did not cease in the apostolic era, but has persisted throughout the various generations of Christendom in isolated individuals or group revivals. The direct antecedents of the present movement are to be seen in the nineteenth and early twentieth century revivals. Such claims of apostolic succession or recovery must of necessity be investigated. Naturally, the mere demonstration of the reality of the phenomenon in different periods cannot in itself prove the reality or Biblical genuineness of the phenomenon today. Neither would the absence of genuine occurrences in the past preclude the possibility of such occurrences today. History can only relate what did or what did not happen. It can neither provide an absolute test for reality or genuineness nor provide a standard for faith and practice. In all spiritual experiences, the Holy Scriptures alone provide the basis for doctrine and life. The Bible must sit in judgment upon history, not vice versa. Nevertheless, with this perspective in mind, a historical knowledge of the tongues movement should be helpful.

Non-Christian Religions

Glossolalia is not unique to the Christian religion. Reports of its occurrence are found in non-Christian religions and philosophies, both past and present. Such reports may be completely or partially true, or totally false. It is impossible to make such an historical judgment. The evidence must be accepted as is. Even if the phenomenon and its report are true, this does not demonstrate absolute identity with either the Biblical glossolalia or the present tongues movement. Biblical glossolalia had its source in God, whereas non-Christian glossolalia, if true, had its source in Satan. The main purpose of this section is to show that the phenomenon of speaking in tongues can be performed or simulated by human or satanic activity. If it could be done in the past, it can likewise be done today in this way. The experience, itself, cannot be the test of its source.

Report of Wenamon

The "Report of Wenamon" gives the most ancient account of frenzied religious speech. It was written about 1100 B.C. from Byblos on the coast of Syro-Palestine. In this report a young worshiper of Amon became possessed by a god and spoke in an ecstatic language. The text reads: "Now, when he sacrificed to his gods . . . the god seized one of his noble youths, making him frenzied, so that he said: 'Bring the god hither! Bring the messenger of Amon who hath him. Send him and let him go.' "[1] This frenzy continued throughout the night.

A few observations are in order here. First, the man spoke frenzied speech which may or may not have been another language. Second, this was a religious phenomenon because the man was engaged in worship. Third, his god considered him worthy of protection and respect. Finally, his frenzied speech was the direct result of his possession and control of or by a god.

Dialogues of Plato

In his dialogues, the great Greek philosopher, Plato (429-347 B.C.) revealed an acquaintance with religious, ecstatic speech. In the *Phaedrus*,[2] he wrote about certain families that were engaged in holy prayers, rites, and inspired utterances. The participants were possessed individuals and out of their minds (loss of control of mental faculties, but not insanity). The usage of these religious exercises even brought physical healing to the worshiper. Plato called prophecy madness and identified madness as a divine gift. He said that the prophetess of Delphi and the priestess at Dodona when out of their senses conferred great benefits upon certain individuals, but when in their senses few or none.

In the *Ion*,[3] Plato stated that good poets compose their poems

---

[1] George A. Barton, *Archaeology and the Bible* (Philadelphia: American Sunday School Union, 1916), p. 353.
[2] Plato, "Dialogues of Plato," trans. Benjamin Jowett, Vol. VII of *Great Books of the Western World*, ed. R. M. Hutchins (Chicago: Encyclopaedia Brittanica, Inc., 1952), sec. 244.
[3] *Ibid.*, sec. 533-34.

not by art, but because they are inspired and possessed. They are not in their right minds because God takes away their minds and uses them as his ministers. God speaks through diviners and holy prophets while they are in a state of unconsciousness. In the inspired utterance, God is the speaker, not the man. He also compared the poets to the Corybantian revellers who became ecstatic in both utterance and action and to the Bacchic maidens of the Dionysian cult.

In the *Timaeus*,[4] Plato stated that when a man receives the inspired word, either his intelligence is enthralled in sleep or he is demented by some distemper or possession. This person (diviner) cannot remember what he has said. These utterances are accompanied by visions which he cannot judge either. Thus, interpreters or prophets are needed to expound the dark sayings of the diviner.

Certain facts must be noted about Plato's observations. First, the speaker of inspired utterances had no control over his mental faculties. Second, he did not understand what was said. Third, there was the need of interpretation by another. Fourth, visions and healing accompanied the speaking. Finally, the person was under divine possession.

Virgil

In his *Aeneid*,[5] Virgil (70-19 B.C.) described the Sibylline priestess on the isle of Delos. She attained her ecstatic state and speech in a haunted cave where drafts and winds made weird sounds and music. When she became unified in spirit with the god Apollo, she began to speak with tongues, sometimes understood and sometimes incoherent.

Pythoness of Delphi

Chrysostom, the great church father, described the Pythoness in this way:

> . . . this same Pythoness then is said, being a female, to sit at times upon the tripod of Apollo astride, and thus the evil spirit ascending from beneath and entering the lower part of her body, fills the woman with madness, and she with dishevelled hair begins to play

---

[4] *Ibid.*, sec. 71-72.
[5] Virgil, "Aeneid," trans. James Rhoades, Vol. XIII of *Great Books of the Western World*, ed. R. M. Hutchins (Chicago: Encyclopaedia Britannica, Inc., 1952), book VI.

the bacchanal and to foam at the mouth, and thus being in a frenzy to utter the words of her madness.[6]

Because of her ability to produce ecstatic utterances under divine inspiration and possession, she was frequently worshiped and consulted for advice and predictions. Martin added: "Priests were apparently in attendance to catch her every utterance, and to interpret her cries and babblings whenever they ceased to be coherent."[7]

Mystery Religions

In the Graeco-Roman world, there were many mystery religions or cults. Among them were the Osiris cult which originated in Egypt, the Mithra cult which began in Persia, and the Eleusinian, Dionysian, and Orphic cults which started in Thrace, Macedonia and Greece. Although there is little evidence for glossolalia in the records of these cults, Martin believed that there were good reasons for assuming that such ecstatic speech was prevalent among them.[8] First, the entire system of beliefs, initiatory rites, and religious practices was centered in the concept of spirit possession or identification. Second, the Christian terms for glossolalia (*pneuma* and *lalein glossais*) came from the Greek vernacular which existed long before the New Testament was written. Third, in the account, *De Dea Syria*, Lucian of Samosata (A.D. 120-198) described a clear case of glossolalia uttered by the itinerant devotees of the Syrian goddess, Juno, stationed at Bambyce or Hieropolis in Syria.

Kittel added that comparable phenomena could be found in the divinatory manticism of the Delphic Phrygia, of the Bacides, and of the Sybils.[9] Concerning worship of the occult and magic, he wrote:

> The unintelligible lists of magical names and letters in the magic pap. (*voces mystical*), which are used in the invoking and conjuring of gods and spirits, may also be analogous to this obscure and meaningless speaking with tongues. With these mystical divine names etc., in which there are echoes of all the various oriental languages, we may certainly couple the view that they derive from supraterrestrial tongues used by the gods and spirits in heaven, each class having its peculiar *phone* or *dialektos*.[10]

---

[6] Chrysostom, "Homilies on First Corinthians," trans. T. W. Chambers, Vol. XII of *The Nicene and Post-Nicene Fathers*, ed. Philip Schaff (First series; New York: The Christian Literature Company, 1889), Hom. 29. 2.
[7] Ira J. Martin, 3rd, *Glossolalia in the Apostolic Church* (Berea, Ky.: Berea College Press, 1960), p. 80.
[8] *Ibid.*, pp. 79-80.
[9] Gerhard Kittell, *Theological Dictionary of the New Testament*, trans. Geoffrey W. Bromiley (Grand Rapids: Wm. B. Eerdmans Publishing Company, 1964), I, 722.
[10] *Ibid.*, I, 723.

Present Occurrences

Stolee reported that ecstatic speech is found in Mohammedanism.[11] The dervishes of Persia constantly utter the name of Allah, accompanied by violent shaking of the body and trances which issue in foaming at the mouth. These violent motions lead to physical exhaustion and partial unconsciousness. During this period of ecstasy, they preach moral sermons.

The Eskimos of Greenland are reported to have engaged in glossolalia.[12] Their religious services are led by the angakok, the medicine man or priest. In these services, there is a definite attempt to get in touch with the nether world. The services are characterized by drum beating, singing, dancing, and nudity of both men and women. Peter Freuchen in his book, *Arctic Adventure*, observed glossolalia in this way:

> Suddenly one of the men, Krisuk, went out of his head. Unable to contain himself to the regular rhythm of the service he leapt to his feet crying like a raven and howling like a wolf. In ecstasy he and the girl, Ivaloo, began to yell in a tongue I could not understand. . . . Certainly it was not the usual Eskimo language . . . and if there is such a thing as speaking in tongues I heard it then.[13]

V. Raymond Edman, chancellor of Wheaton College, gave these accounts of contemporary pagan glossolalia in Tibet and China:

> One of our Wheaton graduates who was born and reared on the Tibetan border tells of hearing the Tibetan monks in their ritual dances speak in English with quotations from Shakespeare, with profanity like drunken sailors, or in German or French, or in languages unknown. Quite recently a retired missionary of the China Inland Mission told of the same experience.[14]

Summary

Occurrences of glossolalia among non-Christians have been reported by both pagan and Christian writers. The similarities of these instances to Biblical glossolalia are quite apparent. The person was engaged in religious worship; he was controlled by a divine being; he lost control of his mental faculties; he spoke in a different language, and there was need for interpretation. However,

---

[11] H. J. Stolee, *Speaking in Tongues* (Minneapolis: Augsburg Publishing House, 1963), p. 19.
[12] *Ibid.*, pp. 85-87.
[13] Cited by Stolee, *ibid.*, pp. 86-87.
[14] V. Raymond Edman, "Divine or Devilish?" *Christian Herald* (May, 1964), 16.

one must not conclude that pagan glossolalia evolved into Christian glossolalia or that Christian glossolalia is a refinement of pagan tongue-speaking. The sources are entirely opposite, God and Satan or self. Nevertheless, it must be admitted that Satan can perform this phenomenon. He has done it in the past; he may be doing it today.

The Old Testament

Martin has identified certain instances of prophetic speaking in the Old Testament with the phenomenon of glossolalia.[15] The Spirit of the Lord came upon Eldad and Medad and they prophesied (Num. 11:26-30). The Holy Spirit also came upon Balaam and he spoke. He also saw visions of God and fell into a trance, but with his eyes open (Num. 23:7-10,18-24; 24:3-9,15-24). The sons of the prophets prophesied to the accompaniment of music. Saul joined them, prophesied, and was turned into another man (I Sam. 10:1-13). Later, Saul stripped off his clothes, prophesied, and lay down naked all the night (I Sam. 19:18-24). On Mount Carmel, the prophets of Baal in contending with Elijah called on the name of Baal continually. They leaped, cried aloud, cut themselves, and prophesied (I Kings 18:26-29).

Even though the actions of these various prophets may approximate those of the speaker in tongues, it cannot be demonstrated that these prophets *did* speak in tongues. There is no explicit statement that they did. To say that they did is to impose a New Testament concept upon an Old Testament action.

The New Testament

The first clear references to the Biblical phenomenon of speaking in tongues are to be found in the New Testament. The disciples spoke with other tongues when the Holy Spirit descended on the day of Pentecost (Acts 2:1-13). Cornelius and his household spoke with tongues when they believed the gospel message of Peter (Acts 10:44-48). The twelve disciples of John the Baptist spoke with tongues after receiving the revelation of Christian truth from Paul (Act 19:1-7). The gift of tongues is discussed by Paul in his first letter to the church at Corinth (I Cor. 12-14).

[15] Martin, *op. cit.*, pp. 74-76.

Tongues are mentioned in the great commission recorded by Mark (16:17), but this passage is textually unsound and contestable.[16] Although there is no explicit reference to tongues in the records of the Samaritan revival (Acts 8:5-25) and of Paul's conversion (Acts 9:1-17), advocates of glossolalia feel strongly that the phenomenon did occur then.[17]

Advocates also see the phenomenon in certain distinctive phrases: "they spake the word of God with boldness" (Acts 4:31); "the Spirit itself maketh intercession for us with groanings which cannot be uttered" (Rom. 8:26); "spiritual songs" (Eph. 5:19; cf. I Cor. 14:15); "praying . . . in the Spirit" (Eph. 6:18; cf. I Cor. 14:15); "Quench not the Spirit. Despise not prophesyings" (I Thess. 5:19-20); "If any man speak, let him speak as the oracles of God" (I Pet. 4:11).

Later chapters will contain an exposition of the passages in Mark, Acts, and First Corinthians. The purpose of this section is just to set forth those Biblical areas that mention the phenomenon.

The Ante-Nicene Period (100-325)

This period of church history was a time of persecution, apologetic defense of the faith, and doctrinal formulation. Many outstanding saints lived, ministered, and were martyred during this period. If tongue-speaking did not cease in the apostolic era, there should be evidence of the phenomenon in the lives and the writings of these great church fathers. Donald Gee, an English Pentecostal writer, believes such evidence does exist. Concerning spiritual gifts, he wrote: "Irenaeus, Tertullian, Chrysostom, Augustine, all refer to these gifts as being still existent in their own times."[18] Cleon Rogers gave the opposite viewpoint in his statement: ". . . it is significant that the gift [of tongues] is nowhere alluded to, hinted at, or found in the Apostolic Fathers."[19] Who is right? Let us examine the evidence.

---

[16] Both the external manuscript evidence and the internal content of this passage argue against its genuineness as an integral part of Mark's gospel. Such a weak foundation cannot be used as a prooftext for any doctrine. This subject will be discussed in a later chapter.

[17] The object of Simon's "seeing" (Acts 8:18) is supposed to be the glossolalia of the Samaritan converts. Paul's alleged testimony of tongue-speaking (I Cor. 14:18) is alleged to have started in Acts 9.

[18] Donald Gee, *Concerning Spiritual Gifts* (Springfield, Mo.: The Gospel Publishing House, n.d.), p. 10.

[19] Cleon L. Rogers, Jr., "The Gift of Tongues in the Post Apostolic Church," *Bibliotheca Sacra*, CXXII (April-June, 1965), 134.

Justin Martyr (110-165)

Justin Martyr was the most eminent of the Greek Apologists in the second century. He is called the first Christian philosopher or the first philosophic theologian. He devoted his entire life to the defense of Christianity and died as a martyr. In Ephesus, he made an effort to gain the Jew Trypho and his friends to the Christian faith. In his famous *Dialogue with Trypho*, he wrote: "For the prophetical gifts remain with us, even to the present time. And hence you ought to understand that [the gifts] formerly among your nation have been transferred to us."[20] He later confessed: "Now, it is possible to see amongst us women and men who possess gifts of the Spirit of God. . . ."[21] At first glance, this would appear that the spiritual gifts, including the gift of tongues, were in existence in the time of Justin. However, the extant gifts were those which Israel once had, and it is nowhere stated in the Old Testament that speaking in tongues was a normal or even rare activity of the Israelites. Justin, himself, defined the nature of the gifts that were then present. He related the prophetical gifts to Solomon (spirit of wisdom), to Daniel (spirit of understanding and counsel), to Moses (spirit of might and piety), to Elijah (spirit of fear), and to Isaiah (spirit of knowledge).[22] These gifts cannot be identified with the spiritual gifts of First Corinthians 12.

Irenaeus (120-202)

Irenaeus is called the first and most orthodox of the church fathers. He studied under Polycarp of Smyrna, a pupil of John the Apostle. After some missionary service, he became Bishop of Lyons in France. His refutation of Gnosticism, *Against Heresies*, is regarded as his most important work. In this book, he wrote the following comment upon First Corinthians 2:6:

> . . . terming those persons "perfect" who have received the Spirit of God, and who through the Spirit of God do speak in all languages, as he used Himself also to speak. In like manner we do also hear many brethren in the church, who possess prophetic gifts, and who through the Spirit speak all kinds of languages, and bring to

---

[20] Justin Martyr, "Dialogue with Trypho," Vol. I of *The Ante-Nicene Fathers*, eds. Alexander Roberts and James Donaldson (Grand Rapids: Wm. B. Eerdman's Publishing Co., 1950), sec. 82, p. 240.

[21] *Ibid.*, sec. 88, p. 243.

[22] *Ibid.*, sec. 87. p. 242.

light for the general benefit the hidden things of men, and declare the mysteries of God. . . .[23]

Certain things must be noted about this quotation. First, he does not say that *he* spoke in tongues. Second, his usage of "we hear" indicates a secondhand acquaintance of the phenomenon rather than an eye-witness observation of it. Third, in his description of those who have the prophetic gifts and tongue-speaking, he is probably referring to the Montanists, whose influence was rather strong at this time.

Montanus (126-180)

Montanus was probably the most controversial figure of the second century. He was basically orthodox. He opposed infant baptism and gnosticism and held to the doctrine of the Trinity, the universal priesthood of believers, millenarianism, and asceticism. He identified the revelation of the Paraclete (John 14:16) with the spiritual religion of the Montanists, who called themselves the *pneumatics* or spiritual church in contrast to the psychical or Catholic church. He regarded himself as the inspired organ of the Holy Spirit. His usage of the first person led many to believe that he made himself *to be* the Holy Spirit. Eusebius characterized him in this way:

> . . . a recent convert, Montanus by name, through his unquench-able desire for leadership, gave the adversary opportunity against him. And he became beside himself, and being suddenly in a sort of frenzy and ecstasy, he raved, and began to babble and utter strange things, prophesying in a manner contrary to the constant custom of the Church handed down by tradition from the beginning. Some of those who heard his spurious utterances at that time were indignant, and they rebuked him as one that was possessed, and that was under the control of a demon, and was led by a deceitful spirit, and was dis-tracting the multitude. . . . And he stirred up besides two women, and filled them with the false spirit, so that they talked wildly and unreasonably and strangely, like the person already mentioned.[24]

What can be learned from Montanus? First, he was regarded as heretical and demon-possessed. He may not have been, but this

[23] Irenaeus, "Against Heresies," Vol. I of *The Ante-Nicene Fathers*, eds. Alexander Roberts and James Donaldson (Grand Rapids: Wm. B. Eerdmmans Publishing Co., 1950), V. 6.1, p. 531.
[24] Eusebius, "Church History," trans. A. C. McGiffert, Vol. I of *The Nicene and Post-Nicene Fathers*, eds. Philip Schaff and Henry Wace (second series; Grand Rapids: Wm. B. Eerdmans Publishing Co., 1961), V. 16, p. 231.

was the evaluation of the Christians in that day. Second, his prophesying and tongue-speaking were contrary to the known procedures of that day. Third, his claim to be the exclusive mouthpiece of the Holy Spirit and his physical actions hardly conform to the Biblical standard.

Tertullian (160-220)

This North African church father is regarded as the father of Latin theology. Converted in middle age, he later joined the Montanists. He labored in Carthage as a Montanist presbyter and author. His belief in the continued existence of spiritual gifts is seen in this statement: "For, seeing that we acknowledge spiritual *charismata*, or gifts, we too have merited the attainment of the prophetic gift. . . ."[25] He then described a woman who had gifts of revelation, ecstatic visions, talks with angels and with God, gifts of healing, and understanding of some men's hearts. In his dispute with Marcion, he wrote:

> Let Marcion then exhibit, as gifts of his god, some prophets, such as have not spoken by human sense, but with the Spirit of God, such as have both predicted things to come, and have made manifest the secrets of the heart; let him produce a psalm, a vision, a prayer—only let it be by the Spirit, in an ecstasy that is, in a rapture, whenever interpretation of tongues has occurred to him. . . . Now all these signs (of spiritual gifts) are forthcoming from my side without any difficulty, and they agree, too, with the rules, and the dispensations, and the instructions of the Creator; therefore without doubt the Christ, and the Spirit, and the apostle, belong severally to my God.[26]

As a Montanist, it is to be expected that Tertullian would embrace the spiritual gifts, including tongue-speaking. On the technical side, it may be stated that Tertullian does not say that he, himself, had spoken in tongues. That he did may be quite probable, but an explicit statement is lacking. Augustine stated that Tertullian later left the Montanists and founded a new sect which was later reconciled to the Catholic congregation at Carthage.[27] If this be so, it may be that Tertullian became disenchanted with the pneumatic excesses of the Montanists.

[25] Tertullian, "A Treatise on the Soul," trans. Peter Holmes, Vol. III of *The Ante-Nicene Fathers*, eds. Alexander Roberts and James Donaldson (Grand Rapids: Wm. B. Erdmans Publishing Co., 1951), sec. 9, p. 188.
[26] *Ibid.*, "Against Marcion," V. 8, p. 477.
[27] Cited by Philip Schaff, *History of the Christian Church* (Grand Rapids: Wm. B. Eerdmans Publishing Co., 1952), II, 420-21.

Origen (185-254)

Origen was no doubt the greatest Christian scholar of his age. He was the most gifted, the most industrious, and the most cultivated of all the ante-Nicene fathers. He became president of the catechetical school at Alexandria. In his refutation of Celsus' attacks against Christianity, he gave to the Christian world one of the most valuable pieces of apologetic literature. These words of Celsus are often used to show the presence of tongue-speaking at that time: "To these promises are added strange, fanatical, and quite unintelligible words, of which no rational person can find the meaning: for so dark are they, as to have no meaning at all . . ."[28] However, these "unintelligible words" do not refer to ecstatic tongue-speaking, but to the difficult prophecies in the Old Testament. In refutation, Origen wrote: ". . . but we have according to our ability, in our commentaries on Isaiah, Ezekiel, and some of the twelve minor prophets, explained literally and in detail what he calls 'those fanatical and utterly unintelligible passages.' "[29]

In another place he wrote about the continuance of some New Testament signs:

> Moreover, the Holy Spirit gave signs of His presence at the beginning of Christ's ministry, and after His ascension He gave still more; but since that time these signs have diminished, although there are still traces of His presence in the few who have had their souls purified by the Gospel, and their actions regulated by its influence.[30]

These signs could not include glossolalia because Christ or His apostles did not speak in tongues while He was upon the earth. They must refer to instances of divine healing which were definitely decreasing.

The Nicene and Post-Nicene Period (311-600)

This was a period of ecclesiastical consolidation and corruption because the Christian religion was accepted by Emperor Constantine and thereby gained the protection of the Roman state. Three significant testimonies to glossolalia arise out of this period: Pachomius, Chrysostom, and Augustine.

---

[28] Origen, "Against Celsus," trans. Frederick Crombie, Vol. IV of *The Ante-Nicene Fathers*, eds. Alexander Roberts and James Donaldson (Grand Rapids: Wm. B. Eerdmans Publishing Co., 1951), sec. 7.9.
[29] *Ibid.*, sec. 7.11.
[30] *Ibid.*, sec. 7.8.

Pachomius (292-348)

Pachomius was the founder of a society of monks on the island of Tabennae in the Nile in Upper Egypt. Legend states that an angel communicated to him his strict mode of life in which he never ate a full meal after his conversion and he slept fifteen years sitting on a stone. His monks always ate in silence and communicated their wants by signs. Concerning his miracles, Schaff wrote: "Tradition ascribes to him all sorts of miracles, even the gift of tongues and perfect dominion over nature, so that he trod without harm on serpents and scorpions and crossed the Nile on the backs of crocodiles."[31] In this context, it would be difficult to say whether Pachomius ever spoke in tongues. Walking unharmed upon snakes and scorpions and using crocodiles for water transportation are certainly incompatible with Biblical miracles.

Chrysostom (345-407)

John Chrysostom was the greatest expositor and preacher of the Greek church. He is quoted more than any other father by modern commentators. Starting out as a monk, he became a deacon and a presbyter at Antioch, and later became the patriarch of Constantinople. In his commentary upon spiritual gifts (I Cor. 12:1-2), he wrote: "This whole place is very obscure: but the obscurity is produced by our ignorance of the facts referred to and by their cessation, being such as then used to occur but now no longer take place."[32] Here is a categorical statement. At least, by the time of Chrysostom, glossolalia had disappeared from the church.

Augustine (354-430)

Augustine was the intellectual head of the North African and Western churches of his time. His doctrine influenced the Roman Catholic church until the time of Thomas Aquinas. He ably defended orthodoxy against Manichaeanism, Donatism, and Pelagianism. In his debate with the Donatists, he affirmed that the Holy Spirit was received without speaking in tongues but rather

[31] Schaff, *op. cit.*, III, 197.
[32] Chrysostom, *op. cit.*, Hom. 29.1.

with the implantation of divine love.[33] The temporary significance of glossolalia is more clearly seen in his commentary on First John:

> In the earliest time, "the Holy Ghost fell upon them that believed: and they spake with tongues," which they had not learned, "as the Spirit gave them utterance." These were signs adapted to the time. For there behooved to be that betokening of the Holy Spirit in all tongues, to shew that the Gospel of God was to run through all tongues over the whole earth. That thing was done for a betokening, and it passed away.[34]

Augustine definitely regarded glossolalia as a temporary phenomenon, limited to the apostolic era. Tongue-speaking was not in existence in his day, nor did he expect its recurrence.

Summary

In the three centuries that followed the apostolic era, there are only two references to tongue-speaking (Montanus and Tertullian who was a Montanist). The fact that Montanism reflected a false, egotistical view of pneumatology can hardly argue for the genuineness of Biblical glossolalia in that period. Therefore, there are no genuine cases of glossolalia in the post-apostolic era. Speaking in tongues had definitely ceased. The testimonies of Justin Martyr, Irenaeus, Origen, Chrysostom, and Augustine confirm this conclusion.

Rogers drew some significant conclusions from the silence of the apostolic fathers on the subject of tongue-speaking.[35] First, some of the fathers wrote from and to churches where the gift had been practiced in New Testament times, and yet, there is no mention of the existence of glossolalia in their time. Nothing is found in the letter of Clement of Rome to the church at Corinth nor in the letter of Ignatius to the church at Ephesus. Second, the fathers lived in cities and wrote to cities in every significant area of the Roman Empire. If glossolalia had been widespread and in existence, it would have been alluded to or mentioned in some way. Third, the fathers wrote on every major New Testament doctrine, and

---

[33] Augustine, "On Baptism, Against the Donatists," trans. J. R. King, Vol. IV of *The Nicene and Post-Nicene Fathers*, ed. Philip Schaff (first series, Buffalo: The Christian Literature Co., 1887), III, 16-21.

[34] Augustine, "Ten Homilies on the First Epistle of John," trans. H. Browne, Vol. VII of *The Nicene and Post-Nicene Fathers*, ed. Philip Schaff (New York: The Christian Literature Company, 1888), VI. 10.

[35] Rogers, *op. cit.*, pp. 134-36.

yet, there is no mention of tongues. Fourth, in many of their writings, the fathers sought to show the superiority of Christianity or the normal character of Christianity; yet, glossolalia is not cited as an example. The silence of the apostolic fathers must be regarded as most significant.

The Middle Ages (590-1517)

This was the period of Roman Catholic domination and doctrinal perversion. It has been aptly called the "Dark Ages" because the light of the Scriptures had seemingly gone out. And yet, even from this period come echoes of glossolalia.

Hildegard (1098-1179)

Hildegard was called the great seeress and prophetess, the Sibyl of the Rhine. She was in ill health most of her life. She had many visions, especially during her sicknesses. Miracles and tongue-speaking have been attributed to her. One evidence of the latter is to be seen in her writing "Lingua Ignota": ". . . the manuscript, in eleven folios, which gives a list of nine hundred words of an unknown language, mostly nouns and only a few adjectives, a Latin, and in a few cases a German, explanation, together with an unknown alphabet of twenty-three letters, printed in Pitra."[36]

Vincent Ferrer (1350-1419)

Vincent Ferrer, a Dominican monk, was reported to have seen an apparition of Christ accompanied by St. Dominic and St. Francis. This experience led to a miraculous cure of a death-sickness. He carried on an extensive miracle-performing and preaching ministry in western Europe. Concerning his preaching, *The Catholic Encyclopedia* stated:

> It would be difficult to understand how he could make himself understood by the many nationalists he evangelized, as he could speak only Limousin, the language of Valencia. Many of his biographers hold that he was endowed with the gift of tongues, an opinion supported by Nicholas Clemangis, a doctor of the University of Paris, who heard him preach.[37]

[36] "Hildegard," *The Catholic Encyclopedia* (New York: The Encyclopedia Press, Inc., 1913), VII, 352.
[37] "Vincent Ferrer," *The Catholic Encyclopedia* (New York: The Encyclopedia Press, Inc., 1913), XV, 438.

The Reformation (1517-1648)

This, of course, was the period of doctrinal revival. Through the ministries of Luther, Calvin, Zwingli, and Knox, the truth of "justification by faith" was re-discovered and presented. There was a change from ritualism to Bible study and simple worship, and yet, there was no attempt to recover glossolalia. However, it is reported that some did speak in tongues.

Martin Luther (1483-1546)

Martin Luther was *the* great reformer. His defense of the faith against the threats of the papacy and the empire is admired by all. Thomas Zimmerman, general superintendent of the Assemblies of God, contended that Luther also spoke in tongues. He cited this statement from Erich Sauer's *History of the Christian Church*: "Dr. Martin Luther was a prophet, evangelist, speaker in tongues and interpreter, in one person, endowed with all the gifts of the Holy Spirit."[38] However, no statement from Luther's own writings is cited as proof for this claim. Sauer may have been referring to Luther's ability to read and to speak German, Latin, Greek, and Hebrew. Brumback, an advocate of glossolalia, recognized this possibility when he wrote: "We have not been able to determine the author's conception of the nature of tongues, and therefore we would hesitate to enter this quotation as conclusive evidence."[33]

Francis Xavier (1506-1552)

Although no reformer, Xavier was a significant figure of the reformation period. It is claimed that he performed miracles and spoke in tongues. However, as a Roman Catholic missionary to the Orient, he devoted his entire first year to learning the Japanese language. When he was able to express himself, he then began to preach.

Summary

To the persons listed under the Middle Ages and the Reformation could be added the names of Louis Bertrand (1526-1581)

---

[38] Thomas F. Zimmerman, "Plea for the Pentecostalists," *Christianity Today*, VII (January 4, 1963), 12.
[39] Carl Brumback, *What Meaneth This?* (Springfield, Mo.: The Gospel Publishing House, 1947), p. 92.

and many other Catholic saints. However, this is unnecessary because their experiences are similar in character to those listed. There is a definite question as to whether the phenomenon of tongue-speaking did occur in these periods. The claims may also be false. Schaff, an outstanding church historian, concluded:

> What may be claimed for St. Bernard, St. Vincent Ferrer, and St. Francis Xavier is not a miraculous heteroglossolalia, but an eloquence so ardent, earnest, and intense, that the rude nations which they addressed in Latin or Spanish imagined they heard them in their mother tongue. . . . Not one of these saints claimed the gift of tongues or other miraculous powers, but only their disciples or later writers.[40]

The tendency of Roman Catholicism to elevate and to venerate their saints must always form the background for any evaluation of their claims to miracles, whether they be healings or tongue-speaking. For this reason, any claim to glossolalia from Catholic sources must be regarded as suspect.

The Post-Reformation Period (1648-1900)

This is the period of Protestant advance, from the Reformation to the Twentieth Century. During this time, "Christianity" spread throughout the world, including America. This period was also marked by the development of cults and sects which sprang up spontaneously or were the result of church splits or dissatisfaction. In many groups, speaking in tongues became an integral part of their worship services.

Cevenal Prophets

During the latter part of the seventeenth and early part of the eighteenth centuries, great persecution broke out against the French Huguenots in the southeastern part of France. In the midst of this tribulation, ecstatic experiences including prophesying and tongue-speaking broke out among the people. Kelsey described the outbreak in this fashion:

> The first occurrence of tongues grew out of the prophetic utterence of a ten-year old, Isabeau Vincent, who had fled from the mistreatment of her father and had seen the king's soldiers bayonet women and children worshipping together in their own church. In an ecstatic experience she called for repentance. . . .

---

[40] Schaff, *op. cit.*, I, 240-41. Proof for Schaff's conclusion will also be found here.

Soon children all over the Cevennes were seized by the spirit and prophesied. Children as young as three were known to have exhorted the people in religious discourses. Adults, too, were seized by the spirit and found themselves speaking the words of French they did not understand.[41]

Their physical actions were quite excessive.[42] They fell backwards with the body extended at full length upon the ground. Their bodies went through many contortions including the heaving of the chest and the inflation of the stomach. When their physical actions ceased, they began to prophesy, exhorting the people to repentance and denouncing the Roman Catholic church.

Jansenists

The Jansenists, started by Cornelius Jansen, were a reform element within the Roman Catholic Church in the seventeenth century. Experience, not reason, was their guide. They were opposed to the teaching of justification by faith. They believed that the relationship of a person to God was only possible in and through the Catholic Church. Glossolalia has been attributed to this group which was later condemned by Rome.

Quakers

The Quakers were started in England during the seventeenth century by George Fox (1624-1691). His aim was to promote the revival of primitive Christianity. He stated that the "Inner Light" was in every man. There was no need for an ordained ministry. They sat in silence in their services until God revealed Himself directly to someone. The Bible was regarded as inspired by God, but it was only a secondary rule, subordinate to the Holy Spirit and to the "Inner Light." Experience therefore sat in judgment upon the Bible, rather than vice versa. It is reported that speaking in tongues took place among the Quakers.

Irvingites

Edward Irving (1792-1834) was a Scotch Presbyterian who was greatly interested in eschatology. This interest was caused

---

[41] Morton T. Kelsey, *Tongue Speaking* (Garden City, N. Y.: Doubleday and Company, Inc., 1964), pp. 52-53.

[42] Robert Chandler Dalton, *Tongues Like As of Fire* (Springfield, Mo.: The Gospel Publishing House, 1945), p. 19.

partially by the French Revolution which had provoked in England a strong interest in apocalyptic thought and was increased through Bible studies in the home of Henry Drummond. He was also noted for his heretical belief in the sinful substance of the body of Christ.

Speaking in tongues broke out among his parishioners in their homes and later in his church services. The Irvingites distinguished between the Pentecostal glossolalia in foreign languages and the Corinthian glossolalia in ecstatic, unknown languages.[43] They only practiced the latter. One premillennial covenant writer has even ascribed the origin of the pretribulation rapture view to a tongue utterance within the Irvingite church.[44]

A later development of the Irvingites was the Catholic Apostolic Church. It restored the position of twelve apostles and degenerated into a distorted Catholicism, embracing such rites as transubstantiation, extreme unction, candles, incense, and holy water.

Shakers

The Shakers, an American celibate and communistic sect, began during the Quaker revival of 1747. Their main leader was "Mother" Ann Lee (1736-1784). Her false teachings included: (1) God, angels, and spirits were both male and female; (2) Jesus Christ was not the incarnate God-man; (3) The second coming was fulfilled in Mother Ann; and (4) Christ's kingdom on earth began with the Shaker church. Ann Lee claimed that she could speak in seventy-two languages. Dollar described one such utterance: "The gift of tongues was also accompanied by times of unspeakable joy and dancing during which many of the hymns of the movement were composed, although made up of unintelligible and unheard of words."[45]

Mormons

Mormonism, established by Joseph Smith (1805-1844), denies salvation by the grace of God, the Trinity, the absolute authority of the Scriptures, and the reality of hell. However, the seventh

---

[43] Schaff, *op. cit.*, I, 237. Schaff observed this latter phenomenon in an Irvingite congregation in New York. The words were unknown; the speakers were unconscious and without control of the tongue.

[44] J. Barton Payne, *The Imminent Appearing of Christ* (Grand Rapids: Wm. B. Eerdmans Publishing Co., 1962), p. 32.

[45] George W. Dollar, "Church History and the Tongues Movement," *Bibliotheca Sacra*, CXX (October-December, 1963), 320.

article of faith of the Latter-day Saints states that they "believe in the gift of tongues, prophecy, revelation, visions, healing, interpretation of tongues, etc."[46]

Various Revivals

The phenomenon of speaking in tongues has been reported to have taken place among the Readers in Sweden (1841-1843), during the Irish revivals (1859), and among early Methodists.[47] The nineteenth century has produced isolated testimonies of those who spoke in tongues without recognizing the significance of the event.[48] Some have claimed that both Moody and Finney, the great evangelists, spoke in tongues when they received the baptism of the Holy Spirit.[49] However, such evidence for this claim is poor.[50] There is no record that Finney or Moody engaged in tonguespeaking. Tongue meetings may have started as the result of their meetings without their sanction or knowledge, but this does not mean that they actively promoted the phenomenon.

Summary

The Post-Reformation period was a time of confusion. Glossolalia appeared, but in the strangest places. Children as young as three years allegedly spoke in tongues. The physical convulsions are hardly in harmony with the Biblical standard of self-control. Glossolalia was totally unrelated to orthodox beliefs. Roman Catholics, Mormons, and false sects (Quakers, Irvingites, Shakers) all reported glossolalia as a part of their church life. Again, it would be difficult to prove that these instances of phenomenon constituted a revival of Biblical tongue-speaking. There are too many discrepancies.

The Modern Period (1900-   )

The contemporary tongues movement among historic, denominational churches has its foundation and heritage in the Pentecostal

[46] Cited by Klaude Kendrick, *The Promise Fulfilled* (Springfield, Mo.: Gospel Publishing House, 1961), p. 24.

[47] Schaff, *op. cit.*, I, 237.

[48] Stanley Howard Frodsham, *With Signs Following* (Springfield, Mo.: Gospel Publishing House, 1946), pp. 7-17. This book is devoted to a historical description of the Pentecostal revival throughout the world.

[49] *Ibid.*, pp. 9-10. Also Jerry Jensen, *Baptists and the Baptism of the Holy Spirit* (Los Angeles: Full Gospel Businessmen's Fellowship International, 1963), p. 2.

[50] Brumback, *loc. cit.* This Pentecostalist writer denies the evidential value of such claims.

denominations. These denominations are primarily a development of the Twentieth Century. This is the period of Pentecostal birth, growth, and expansion.

Causes of Pentecostalism

What caused the outbreak of modern tongue-speaking and the subsequent establishment of Pentecostal churches? Various answers have been given. First, there was a breakdown of strong orthodoxy after the Civil War. As a result, evolution and the philosophy of Horace Bushnell's *Christian Nurture*[51] invaded and conquered the established churches. Second, the industrial revolution produced moral corruption and labor-management problems. Third, the reaction to this spiritual, moral, and economic breakdown was the rise of the Holiness Movement. Methodism and camp meetings stressed Christian holiness and perfection (second blessing). This doctrine found a ready acceptance in the rural and frontier areas of the United States. Fourth, key Pentecostal leaders (Spurling, Tomlinson, Parham) began to promote their distinctive position actively. Fifth, a sympathetic and tolerant attitude toward the Pentecostal movement developed among the leaders of American orthodoxy. This classic statement by A. B. Simpson, a leader of the Christian and Missionary Alliance, will serve as an example:

> We believe the scriptural teaching to be that the gift of tongues is one of the gifts of the Spirit, and that it may be present in the normal Christian assembly, as a sovereign bestowal of the Holy Spirit upon such as He wills. We do not believe that there is any scriptural evidence for the teaching that speaking in tongues is the sign of having been filled with the Holy Spirit, nor do we believe that it is the plan of God that all Christians should possess the gift of tongues. This gift is one of many gifts and is given to some for the benefit of all. The attitude toward the gift of tongues held by pastor and people should be "Seek not, forbid not." This we hold to be the part of wisdom for this hour.[52]

Simpson, himself, and his movement were not marked by glossolalia; however, certain individuals within the denomination did attempt to recover the spiritual gifts. Pentecostalists took advantage of this tolerant attitude and emphasized the "forbid not" command

---

[51] There is no need for spontaneous conversion. People gradually become Christians through education, not through an instantaneous event of regeneration. People are basically good, not evil.

[52] Cited by Kelsey, *op. cit.*, p. 75. Simpson said this in 1907. It was reaffirmed in the *Alliance Witness*, the official organ of the CMA, in 1963 (May 1, 1963, Vol. 98, No. 9, p. 19).

and neglected the "seek not" one. They accepted the thesis that the gift of tongues is sovereignly bestowed, but rejected the view that it is not the sign of the baptism or the infilling of the Holy Spirit.

Founders of Pentecostalism

Movements are men. The beginnings of modern Pentecostalism are marked by key men who gave direction and impetus to its distinctive position. There were many; only a few are mentioned here.

Richard G. Spurling, a licensed minister and pastor of the Baptist church near the community of Cokercreek in Monroe County, Tennessee, became dissatisfied with the established churches and formed his own group in 1886. Later, in Cherokee County, North Carolina, he led a revival that was marked by an extensive outburst of speaking in tongues (1896). His teaching and revival services assisted the establishment of the Church of God, led by the Tomlinson family.[53]

Charles F. Parham (1873-1929) has been called "the father of the modern Pentecostal movement."[54] He established the Bethel Healing Home (1898) and the Bethel Bible College (1900) in Topeka, Kansas. The student body (about forty) was asked to research the question, "What is the Bible evidence of the baptism of the Holy Ghost?" There was unanimous agreement that speaking in tongues was this evidence. From this time (Fall, 1900), there was a concerted effort to receive the baptism of the Holy Spirit with its evidence of tongue-speaking. One of the students, Agnes Ozman, spoke in tongues on January 1, 1901. The significance of this event has been pointed out by Kendrick: "Although Agnes Ozman was not the first person in modern times to speak 'in tongues,' she was the first person to have received such an experience as a result of specifically seeking a baptism in the Holy Spirit with the expectation of speaking in tongues."[55] Henceforth, Pentecostalists were to teach that the Baptism of the Holy Spirit was an experience to

---

[53] For further information, see Charles W. Conn, *Like a Mighty Army Moves the Church of God*, 1886-1955 (Cleveland, Tenn.: Church of God Publishing House, 1955), 300 pages.
[54] Kendrick, *op. cit.*, p. 37.
[55] *Ibid.*, p. 53.

be sought and to be verified in tongues. For this reason, the experience of Agnes Ozman has been called the beginning of the modern Pentecostal revival.

In 1905, Parham established the Houston Bible School in Houston, Texas. One of his convinced students was W. J. Seymour, a Negro Holiness preacher. Seymour was invited to preach at a Nazarene church in Los Angeles, California. He was later locked out of this Nazarene church because of his extreme holiness preaching. He then held meetings in a home at 214 North Bonnie Brae Street. On April 9, 1906, seven received the baptism of the Holy Spirit and spoke in tongues. Many people were then attracted to the meetings by the shouts of praise that came out of the building. The meetings were moved to 312 Azusa Street which later became the famous Azusa Street Mission. The meetings lasted, night and day, for three years. From this place, the teaching of Pentecostalism spread rapidly across the land. What characterized these services? They were led by both male and female preachers. The Spirit of God was *seen* falling upon people.[56] Gaebelein copied this excerpt from the Azusa Street Mission organ: "The power of God fell and every one was caught up in the Spirit and saw visions of God. Several had a vision of the Savior. He held a book in his hand. They saw the nailprints *and the blood trickling down* while he wrote their names in the book with His fingers with the blood that ran from His pierced hand."[57] One would wonder whether this was an hallucination rather than a vision. Are people able to see God and Christ today? Is Christ presently bleeding in heaven?

Growth of Pentecostalism

Certain passages in the Old Testament speak of the rainfall in Palestine in two seasons, the early rain and the latter rain (Hosea 6:3; Joel 2:23). Pentecostalists believe that these passages have a prophetic character. The early rain was Pentecost with its unusual signs and blessings (Acts 2). The latter rain began at the turn of the century and is continuing to fall within the Pentecostal revival and growth. Such a conviction (although built upon a misinterpretation and a misapplication of Scripture) has no doubt given impetus to its growth.

[56] Frodsham, *op. cit.*, p. 37.
[57] Arno C. Gaebelein, "The So-Called Gift of Tongues," *Our Hope*, XIV (July, 1907), 15.

At the first, the Pentecostal assemblies remained isolated from each other, but they soon saw the need for association. Over a dozen Pentecostal denominations have developed. "While some divergence of doctrine exists, one basic position unites Pentecostals— their common belief that 'the baptism in the Holy Spirit' is a distinct experience which all believers may and should have *following* conversion."[58]

The development of Pentecostal congregations led to the Hot Springs, Arkansas, convention in April 2-12, 1914. This then led to the formation of the Assemblies of God, the largest of the Pentecostal groups. Its growth has been marked by Kendrick:[59]

Year	Churches	Membership
1920	1612	91,981
1939	3496	184,022
1949	5950	275,000
1959	8094	505,552

Today, there are over 8409 churches with a membership of 543,003. Churches are located in every state and seventy-three countries. This one example gives clear cause why *Time* called Pentecostalism the "fastest growing church in the hemisphere."[60] It has a great attraction to nominal Roman Catholics of Latin America. Pentecostalists probably outnumber traditional Protestants by four to one in Latin America. In 1948, ten denominations united to form the Pentecostal Fellowship of North America. There is also a world Pentecostal fellowship with an international publication, *Pentecost*, edited by Donald Gee. Their growth is quite apparent.

Current Emphasis

In the past, the distinctives of Pentecostalism were limited to their own groups. However, in recent years, the Pentecostal message has been embraced by members of the established, historic Protestant churches. When did this start? Most observers date the beginning of the current emphasis in the years 1955-1960. The event that proved to be the catalyst of the modern glossolalia movement took place in Van Nuys, California, on April 3, 1960. The

[58] Thomas F. Zimmerman, "The Pentecostal Position," *The Pentecostal Evangel* (Springfield, Mo.), February 10, 1963, p. 2.
[59] Kendrick, *op. cit.*, p. 95. This book gives a history of the modern Pentecostal movement, especially that of the Assemblies of God.
[60] "Fastest-Growing Church in the Hemisphere," *op. cit.*, p. 56.

rector of the St. Mark's Episcopal Church, Dennis Bennett, announced from the pulpit that he had spoken in tongues. This declaration not only shocked his congregation, but received nation-wide publicity and notoriety. This event has been acclaimed as the start of the charismatic renewal in the historic churches, with its emphasis upon the gifts of the Holy Spirit and the gift of tongues in particular. The nature of this movement will be discussed more fully in the next chapter.

Summary

The phenomenon of speaking in tongues is not unique to the Christian religion. Occurrences among pagans have been recorded in the Report of Wenamon, the Dialogues of Plato, and the Aeneid of Virgil. The pythoness of Delphi and the adherents to the mystery religions are alleged to have spoken in tongues. In the Twentieth Century, it has occurred among the Mohammedans, the Eskimos, and the pagans of Tibet and China. Since God is not the source of this glossolalia, these instances show that the phenomenon can be duplicated by Satanic or human effort.

In the Old Testament, there are cases of prophetic speaking accompanied by strange physical actions, but there is no definite indication that tongue-speaking took place.

The first clear instances of Biblical glossolalia are to be found in the New Testament. It was predicted by Jesus (Mark 16:17; but this is contestable) and was experienced by the disciples in Jerusalem (Acts 2), by Cornelius in Caeserea (Acts 10), by the disciples of John the Baptist in Ephesus (Acts 19), and by the church at Corinth (I Cor. 12-14). These passages will be discussed later.

In the post-apostolic era (100-600), speaking in tongues ceased as a normal activity of the believers. Justin Martyr, Irenaeus, Origen, Chrysostom, and Augustine all testified to this fact. The only occurrences of the phenomenon appeared among the Montanists (Montanus and possibly Tertullian) and an ascetic monk, Pachomius. The heretical positions of these men would argue against the genuineness of Biblical glossolalia among them.

During the Middle Ages and the Reformation period (590-1648), certain Roman Catholic saints are alleged to have spoken in tongues. Again, because of the faulty doctrinal foundation of the

Roman Catholic Church and the tendency to exaggerate the accomplishments of their saints, these claims must be rejected. The intense spiritual and doctrinal revival in Europe (Reformation) produced no cases of glossolalia. The reference to Martin Luther is spurious.

The Post-Reformation period (1648-1900) produced a rash of tongue-speaking occurrences. The phenomenon appeared among the Cevenal prophets, Jansenists (Roman Catholic group), Quakers, Irvingites, Shakers, Mormons, and during various revivals in the nineteenth century. None of these groups can be regarded as orthodox in doctrine or life. The nature of their tongue-speaking is not in harmony with the Biblical experiences and regulations.

The twentieth century has seen the birth, the growth, and the influence of modern Pentecostalism. This movement, with its emphasis upon glossolalia, is a force that must be reckoned with. Its nature will be discussed in the next chapter.

CHAPTER III

THE NATURE OF THE MODERN TONGUES MOVEMENT

The contemporary expression of the tongues movement has only been in existence for five to ten years, and yet, it has caused great debate and amazement in both Pentecostal and non-Pentecostal circles, including both liberal and conservative camps. An understanding of the basic nature of this contemporary phenomenon is therefore imperative for every serious Bible student. A study of modern Pentecostalism will not be undertaken as such, but only as it affects the established churches of Protestantism. Once this basic nature has been presented, the contemporary movement can then be evaluated in the light of Scriptural truth to ascertain whether it be of God or not. The purpose of this chapter then is to present the advocates of the contemporary tongues movement, its outreach, its characteristics, its causes, and the subsequent evaluations of this new phenomenon.

Advocates of the Modern Movement

Many groups, religious publications, and key personalities are actively promoting the charismatic renewal among the historic Protestant churches. Whenever the subject of modern glossolalia is discussed, these names are invariably mentioned.

The Full Gospel Business Men's Fellowship International[1] is an organization of businessmen wholly committed to the full gospel message with its emphasis upon the spiritual gifts and the phenomenon of speaking in tongues as the evidence of the baptism of the Holy Spirit. The organization was conceived and founded by Demos Shakarian,[2] a wealthy California businessman, who was encouraged in the idea by Irvine J. Harrison and Oral Roberts.

---

[1] Headquarters are located at 836 S. Figueroa St., Los Angeles, California. The organization is hereafter referred to as the FGBMFI.

[2] The Shakarian family is greatly revered in Pentecostal circles. For over one hundred years, it has been marked by claims of direct prophetic revelation, healing miracles, visions, and tongue-speaking. After leaving Armenia the family had contact with the Azusa Street Mission and one of the first Pentecostal churches in America was established in their home in 1905. For further information, see Thomas R. Nickel, *The Shakarian Story* (Los Angeles: FGBMFI, 1964), 32 pages.

Shakarian presently serves as president of this international organization. A related organization is the World Missionary Assistance Plan (World MAP), a non-denominational Full Gospel Missionary Fellowship composed of "Spirit-filled" missionaries working in the Western hemisphere, the Orient, southeast Asia, India, and Africa. What are the purposes of FGBMFI? Mahoney stated, "I believe one of the specific purposes for FGBMFI is to bridge the gap that has kept the Pentecostal message from the traditional churches."[3] This is true. The FGBMFI, more than any other organization, has reached and won people within the historic churches. How has this been done? First, FGBMFI has sponsored banquets and conventions throughout the country and the world. There are local monthly banquets,[4] and regional, national, and international conventions, held in modern hotel and convention centers. At these affairs, featured speakers are key Pentecostal leaders and both laymen and ministers from the traditional Protestant churches who have received the baptism in the Holy Spirit accompanied by the evidence of tongue-speaking. Many guests from the historic churches are invited to these events and some accept the Pentecostal message as the result of them. These then return to their respective churches and testify to their new experiences. As a result, many churches have wholeheartedly accepted this Pentecostal teaching of the renewal of the spiritual gifts, but others have been divided over it. Concerning the approach of the FGBMFI to non-Pentecostals, Hitt, editor of *Eternity* magazine has candidly observed: "The most polished of public relations techniques have been enrolled to advance the movement. While there is certainly nothing wrong with using modern techniques, the neo-Pentecostalism cannot claim complete spontaneity."[5] The outbreak of tongue-speaking must be seen as the result of a determined attempt by Pentecostals to win church members of historic churches who have grown dissatisfied with their personal spiritual experiences (none, in some cases) and with the empty formalism of their local churches. A second method of promoting the "full gospel" message has been through the printed page. There are three publications printed by the FGBMFI. Their most popular

---

[3] Ralph Mahoney, "Pentecost in Perspective," *Full Gospel Business Men's Voice,* XIII (May, 1965), 4.

[4] The author attended one of these. See Appendix I for description.

[5] Russel T. Hitt, "The New Pentecostalism: An Appraisal," *Eternity,* XIV (July, 1963), 16.

magazine is *Voice*, a monthly publication, which contains testimonies of those who have been "baptized in the Holy Spirit" and announcements of future conventions. *Vision* is a magazine with a special appeal to youth. *View* is a quarterly journal that deals with the charismatic renewal.

Another key group is the Blessed Trinity Society which sponsors Christian Advance meetings throughout the country. A Dutch Reformed minister, Harold Bredesen of Mt. Vernon, New York, is the chairman of the board and a key spokesman, especially on college campuses. David J. du Plessis, a director, is a Pentecostalist from South Africa "who believes he has a call to take the message to ecumenical leaders. In his opinion, the 'Pentecostal revival' within the ecumenical movement may become greater than that outside it. His ecumenical activities have led to a severing of his ministerial relationship with the Assemblies [of God], by the latter."[6] Jean Stone, wife of a Lockheed Aircraft executive, is a board member and the editor of the society's attractive, Episcopal-oriented magazine, *Trinity*, published in Van Nuys, California. She has expressed the purpose of the society in these words: "Many people have yearned to see God pour out His Spirit on the historic churches. . . It was to make it happen that Blessed Trinity Society came into being."[7]

Pentecostal publications (*Abundant Life, The Pentecostal Herald, The Pentecostal Evangel, Miracle Magazine, Pentecostal Holiness Advocate, The Voice of Healing, Pentecost*) are naturally pushing the movement. A well-known, monthly magazine, *Christian Life*, edited by Robert Walker, is actively promoting the charismatic revival.

Pentecostal colleges are raising their academic standards and seeking accreditation in order to enhance their appeal and status. In fact, Oral Roberts University with its Graduate School of Theology (opened in 1965) has been established with the express purposes of furnishing the finest in Christian education and of promoting the charismatic renewal. It is located at Tulsa, Oklahoma.

Outreach of the Modern Movement

To what extent has the modern tongues movement touched

[6] Frank Farrell, "Outburst of Tongues: The New Penetration," *Christianity Today*, VII (September 13, 1963), 6.
[7] Jean Stone, "Would You Like a Christian Advance? *Trinity*, II (Christmastide, 1962-1963), 51. Headquarters for the Society are located at P. O. Box 2422, Van Nuys, California.

the secular and the sacred worlds? Its extent will point out the significance of such a study as this.

Secular World

Leading national publications (*Life, Saturday Evening Post, Time, Newsweek, The National Observer*, etc.) have carried articles on the new Pentecostalism. There has also been radio and television coverage. In fact, there was a special report on speaking in tongues featuring Harold Bredesen on the evening CBS news, Kronkite reporting, April 21, 1965.

Schools and Groups

David J. du Plessis has presented the charismatic message to the International Missionary Council of the World Council of Churches, the Presbyterian World Alliance, Yale Divinity School, Union Theological Seminary (New York), and Princeton Seminary.[8] Homer A. Tomlinson, Bishop and General Overseer of the Church of God, Queens Village, New York, has lectured on tongues in over twenty-two seminaries, including Yale and Harvard, plus Catholic seminaries and Moslem groups.[9] Reports of tongue-speaking have also come from Dartmouth, Fuller Seminary, Westmont College, and Wheaton College.[10] Speaking in tongues apparently has occurred within such conservative groups as the Navigators, the Wycliffe Bible Translators, and the Inter-Varsity Christian Fellowship.

Denominations

Practically all of the major historic denominations have been penetrated and influenced by the new charismatic revival. The Dutch Reformed penetration can be seen in Harold Bredesen, pastor of the First Reformed Church of Mount Vernon, New York. He spends much of his time promoting the charismatic renewal both within and without his denomination.

---

[8] James W. L. Hills, "The New Pentecostalism: Its Pioneers and Promoters," *Eternity*, XIV (July, 1963), 18.
[9] Contained in a letter from Tomlinson to Richard Ruble. Cited by Richard Lee Ruble, "A Scriptural Evaluation of Tongues in Contemporary Theology" (Unpublished Th.D. dissertation, Dallas Theological Seminary, 1964), p. 66.
[10] Farrell, *op. cit.*, pp. 3-4. However, V. R. Edman, Chancellor of Wheaton, denied that there was a tongue awakening at Wheaton, but affirmed that a few students had done so under outside influences. See V. R. Edman, Letter to the Editor, *Christianity Today*, VIII (October 25, 1963), 23.

The impact within the Episcopal denomination[11] has been so strong that officials of the Protestant Episcopal Church and the Assemblies of God have had a mutual conference in order to discuss the ministry of the Holy Spirit today. One outstanding spokesman is Dennis Bennett, the Episcopalian rector whose confession of tongue-speaking at St. Mark's Church in Van Nuys, California, started the charismatic renewal. After being forced to resign, he became rector of the St. Luke's Episcopal Church in Seattle, Washington. He frequently speaks at FGBMFI banquets and conventions and is a contributor of many articles to leading publications.

Many Baptist ministers and laymen have spoken in tongues.[12] This has occurred among members of churches associated with the Southern Baptist Convention, American Baptist Convention, and the Baptist Bible Fellowship. Francis Whiting, a leader within the ABC, has spoken in support of the tongues phenomenon at Northern Baptist Seminary. Howard Ervin, pastor of Emmanuel Baptist Church, Atlantic Highlands, New Jersey, in his tongue-speaking has supposedly spoken to foreign nationals (Japanese, Russian, Spanish) in their own languages. He has also served as a theological consultant to the Oral Roberts Graduate School of Theology.

Presbyterian churches have also been affected.[13] The fashionable Bel Air Presbyterian Church in Los Angeles, pastored by Louis Evans, Jr., has evidenced the phenomenon.[14] A key spokesman has been James Brown, minister of the Upper Octorara United Presbyterian Church in Parkesburg, Pennsylvania. Brown has preached widely in FGBMFI banquets and conventions.

Time reported that at least 260 of the 5239 American Lutheran churches have glossolalia cells.[15] Larry Christenson, key Lutheran minister and tongues enthusiast, has described the existence of the phenomenon among the Evangelical Mary Sisterhood in Darmstadt, West Germany.[16] The sisterhood practices the gifts of the Spirit

---

[11] Jerry Jensen (ed.), *Episcopalians and the Baptism in the Holy Spirit* (Los Angeles: FGBMFI, 1964). This booklet contains testimonies of leading Episcopalians who have spoken in tongues.

[12] Jerry Jensen (ed.), *Baptists and the Baptism of the Holy Spirit* (Los Angeles: FGBMFI, 1963). Contains testimonies of Baptists who have spoken in tongues.

[13] Jerry Jensen (ed.), *Presbyterians and the Baptism of the Holy Spirit* (Los Angeles: FGBMFI, 1963). Contains testimonies of Presbyterians who have spoken in tongues.

[14] Robert Walker, "Church on the Mountaintop," *Christian Life*, XXV (July, 1963), 27-31.

[15] "Taming the Tongues," *Time*, LXXXIV (July 10, 1964), p. 66.

[16] Larry Christenson, "Miracles Are Not Commonplace Here," *Christian Life*, XXVII (June, 1965), 36-37, 52-54.

and private confession. It is also engaged in evangelism, teaching, religious drama, works of charity and mercy, production of religious art, and the publication of Mother Basilea's writings. Mother Basilea, the founder and theologian of the community, has a doctorate in philosophy and psychology. Her major theological influences have been Dietrich Bonhoeffer and Karl Barth. She has given much attention to mystics as Madame Guyon, Benedict of Nursia, and Francis of Assisi.

Methodism has also felt the impact of tongue-speaking.[17] The Hillcrest Christian Church (Disciples of Christ) in Toronto, Canada, has reported that nearly all nine of the spiritual gifts are in evidence within the church. It is claimed that God has revealed Himself to various members and that He has made known His will through dreams and visions.[18] A Russian Orthodox priest claimed that his church has always had speakers in tongues, but they are found in the monasteries, not at the parish level.[19] The phenomenon is not even absent from the Roman Catholic Church. Some Catholic clergy stated to Bennett that the gift of tongues (and others) has been in the Roman Catholic Church throughout her history.[20] Also, one Catholic recently admitted: "Glossolalia is a lot more widespread than most Christians realize. I am a Roman Catholic and for years have found speaking in tongues to be an integral part of my private worship."[21]

The outburst of tongue-speaking is not limited to this country. Reports of the Pentecostal revival come from the Philippines, Japan, Formosa, Sweden, Holland, and South Africa. It is reported that seventy percent of the evangelicals in Poland have received the baptism of the Holy Spirit and have spoken in tongues as the evidence.[22]

Personalities

In addition to those already mentioned, there are others,

---

[17] Jerry Jensen (ed.), *Methodists and the Baptism of the Holy Spirit* (Los Angeles: FGBMFI, 1963). Contains testimonies of Methodists who have spoken in tongues.

[18] Don W. Basham, "I Saw My Church Come Alive," *Christian Life,* XXVI (March, 1965), 37-39.

[19] Dennis Bennett, "The Charismatic Renewal and Liturgy," *View,* II (No. 1, 1965), 1.

[20] *Ibid.*

[21] Michael Callaghan, Letter to the Editor, *Time,* LXXVI (September 5, 1960), 2.

[22] Wesley R. Hurst, Jr., "Upon All Flesh," *The Pentecostal Evangel* (May 2, 1965), p. 11.

well known to both the sacred and the secular worlds, who have
allegedly spoken in tongues. Catherine Marshall LeSourd, authoress
and wife of the late Peter Marshall, is one. Another is Coleen
Townsend Evans, wife of Presbyterian minister Louis Evans and
ex-Hollywood actress who has starred in several Christian films.
Chandler Sterling, the Episcopal Bishop of Montana, has experienced
the phenomenon. So has McCandlish Phillips, reporter for the *New
York Times*, and John Sherrill, staff writer of *Guideposts* magazine.[23]

The wide scope of speaking in tongues within the historic
churches has created a small dilemma for its adherents. At the
present time, these tongue-speakers have remained as loyal members
of their churches. However, their zeal for their new-found experience has caused strife and division within their local churches.
There are several alternative solutions to this problem. They can
stay within their local churches, promote their experiences, and risk
splitting the church or possible excommunication. They can stay
and keep quiet about their experiences. Or, they can leave their
respective churches and identify themselves with Pentecostal assemblies. Only time will reveal what course they will take.

Characteristics of the Modern Movement

In order to understand the nature of the tongues movement,
one needs an accurate cross section of its characteristics. Who is
speaking? Where is it taking place? What other things are happening? What are the results of such experiences? How does one
come to the place where he will speak in tongues?

Participants

In the past, certain generalizations were used in attacking and
refuting the Pentecostal position. Today, these categorical statements must be regarded as false or at the most, partially true.
One classic observation was made by Stegall, an avid student of
Pentecostalism:

> The appeal of Pentecostalism is limited quite clearly to the naive
> and gullible mind which will accept things without investigation. The
> great majority of the followers of the healers are old people, shallow

---

[23] Cited by Lee E. Dirks, " 'Tongues' and the Historic Churches," *The National
Observer*, October 26, 1964. Also, John L. Sherrill, *They Speak With Other Tongues*
(New York: McGraw-Hill Book Company, 1964). This is an autobiographical account
of his advance from curiosity and doubt about tongues to the time that he actually
spoke in tongues. It is receiving wide publicity and circulation from the FGBMFI.

people—people cast aside by society and forgotten by the proud "established churches," to our eternal discredit.[24]

Martin added that only the low intellectual and the low economic groups participate in the phenomenon.[25] Such statements just cannot be made today. The new Pentecostalism has been embraced by wealthy, cultured, and educated people including professors, writers, ministers, doctors, and lawyers.[26] A wide range of personal and denominational backgrounds is represented.

This modern tongue-speaking is taking place everywhere: in homes, in private and public prayer groups, in church services, and in banquet and convention rooms. It is much like the old Pentecostalism and yet, somewhat different. Mrs. Stone expressed these differences:

> . . . less emotion in receiving the gift of tongues after which they are spoken at will—their private use more important than public, more oriented to clergy and professional classes, more Bible-centered as against experience, not separatist, more orderly meetings with strict adherence to Pauline directives, less emphasis on tongues.[27]

However, the old Pentecostalism still persists and is an integral part of the new movement. Dalton, an Assembly of God minister, once classified three groups within Pentecostalism: the orderly group which does everything decently and in order; the offshoot of the orderly group which tries to work up in the flesh what others have in the Spirit; and the group that is all flesh and always has been all flesh.[28] These are no doubt still in existence today.

Concomitants

Quite often, certain unusual things happen before and after the person has spoken in tongues. A physician reported: "When I went to bed, I had no more than pulled the covers over me when the room was filled with a mighty rushing sound, which might be described as wind, and in a few moments tongues of fire."[29] Four

---

[24] Carroll Stegall, Jr., *The Modern Tongues and Healing Movement* (Atlanta, Ga.: By the author, n.d.), p. 53.

[25] Martin, *op. cit.*, pp. 17, 25. However, Jean Stone reported that Martin recanted of this position and accepted the genuineness of the modern phenomenon. See Jean Stone and Harold Bredesen, *The Charismatic Renewal in the Historic Churches* (Van Nuys, Calif.: Blessed Trinity Society, n.d.). Reprint from Trinity, Trinitytide, 1963.

[26] Jerry Jensen (ed.), *Attorneys' Evidence on the Baptism in the Holy Spirit* (Los Angeles: FGBMFI, 1965). Contains impressive testimonies of attorneys who have spoken in tongues.

[27] Cited by Farrell, *op. cit.*, p. 6.

[28] Dalton, *op. cit.*, p. 116.

[29] R. O. McCorkle, "Witness to the World," *Full Gospel Business Men's Voice*, XIII (February, 1965), 23.

months later, this man received the baptism and spoke in tongues after people had "laid their hands on me according to biblical pattern."[30] A Scriptural observation is in order here. Wind and fire were present at Pentecost (Acts 2:2-3), but there was no laying on of hands. At Pentecost, when the wind and fire did occur, the disciples were filled with the Spirit and spoke in tongues (Acts 2:4). This man did not receive the Spirit or speak in tongues *until four months later*. The sound at Pentecost attracted a large crowd (Acts 2:6), but his sound attracted none.

Another person wrote: "Recently, in one of our meetings, at least 20 people in the group smelled the fragrance of perfume and incense."[31] He concluded that this was the result of believers being an *aroma* of life unto life (II Cor. 2:16). This is certainly a novel interpretation of that experience and of that verse. Certainly there is no incident recorded in the Bible where believers smelled the spiritual fragrance of heaven, much less that of one another.

Shaking and physical convulsions are still found associated with tongue-speaking.[32] However, this concomitant is deplored by many. David du Plessis, former General Secretary of the Pentecostal World Conference, wrote:

> I consider it heresy to speak of shaking, trembling, falling, dancing, clapping, shouting, and such like actions as 'manifestations' of the Holy Spirit. These are purely human reactions to the power of the Holy Spirit and frequently hinder, more than help, to bring forth genuine manifestations.[33]

Visions and shocks of electricity that go through the body have also been experienced. John Osteen, a Baptist minister, claimed that he saw Jesus and heard him speak. When he reached out toward Jesus, a million volts of electricity, like two bolts of lightning, struck his hands. He later saw a ball of light which contained "a Man" with an outstretched hand rapidly coming toward him. When he leaped up and backed away in fright, the bubble burst and left the room in darkness. At another time, he saw a vision of a hand thrust out of eternity, holding an Oriental bottle. When the oil was poured

---

[30] *Ibid.*, p. 28.
[31] John Topping, "Hearts Aflame," *Full Gospel Business Men's Voice*, XIII (February, 1965), 6.
[32] The author attended a Pentecostal church service where this took place. See Appendix II.
[33] Cited by Tod W. Ewald, "Aspects of Tongues," *View*, II (No. 1, 1965), 9. These very things were witnessed by the author. See Appendix II.

out, a voice said, "I have anointed your heart to speak to the people on the morrow."[34]

Cho Yonggi, a converted Buddhist and co-pastor of the Assemblies of God evangelistic center in Seoul, gave this account of his healing from tuberculosis:

> I saw the Lord . . . and I said to Him, "Yes, Jesus, I will preach your gospel." I tried to touch His feet. As soon as I touched His clothes, what seemed like a thousand volts of electricity flowed into me and I began to shake. Then strange words came to my mouth and I began to speak in other tongues. When I awakened from this vision, I was a changed man. Right away I went to the hospital and had X-ray pictures taken. There was no sign of my tuberculosis at all.[55]

Frodsham, a Pentecostal historian, reported that young Chinese boys had experienced visions.[36] They danced with angels, walked in the New Jerusalem in the third heaven, played by the streams with the animal pets in the heavenly Eden, enjoyed the fruits, flowers and birds of the restored paradise, visited hell, witnessed the events of the Old Testament, the Gospels, and the book of Revelation, saw their departed loved ones and saw Christ.

Wind, fire, perfume, shaking, physical convulsions, electric shocks, lights, perspiration (from the heat of the Holy Spirit), visions, healings, seeing, hearing and touching Christ—these are the concomitants of speaking in tongues. One searches the New Testament in vain to find such accompaniments to the ministry of the Holy Spirit in the lives of believers at the time they spoke in tongues.

Results

Those who have spoken in tongues have testified to the fact that they now have changed lives. Emotional problems have been stabilized and overcome. Personal sins are faced, confessed, and forsaken. *Time* reported that to participants, speaking in tongues "is good for ending alcoholism, repairing broken marriages and furthering the work of Christ."[37] There is a new interest in the church involving regular attendance, tithing, counselling, and witnessing for Christ. There is a new desire to read and to study the Bible. They have a new sense of divine love and joy which manifests

---

[34] John H. Osteen, "He Heard God Speak," *Baptists and the Baptism of the Holy Spirit* (Los Angeles: FGBMFI, 1963), 8-9.
[35] Hurst, *op. cit.*, pp. 11-12.
[36] Frodsham, *op. cit.*, pp. 131-138.
[37] "Against Glossalalia," *Time*, LXXXI (May 17, 1963), 84.

itself in personal warmth and enthusiastic singing. The experience of speaking in tongues has caused some to worship God more freely and profoundly although they do not understand the words being uttered. Some have experienced both physical and mental healings. "But the most wonderful thing is the conviction of the reality of God and the work of redemption through Christ that dawns in their lives. These folks *know* that they are inheritors of the Kingdom, for they have a foretaste of it in this dynamic fellowship in the Holy Spirit."[38]

All of these are commendable results, but it must be remembered that the results of a spiritual experience do not form the test of the divine genuineness of the experience. Their interpretation as to the cause and the meaning of the experience may be wrong. All experiences must be judged by the Word of God. The end does not justify or reveal the means.

Instructions

How does one come to speak in tongues? Does he suddenly speak without having had previous knowledge of or desire for the phenomenon? Or, does he receive assistance in the form of instructions? The latter is true of the modern tongues movement. Christenson, a Lutheran minister and tongue-speaker, said:

> In order to speak in tongues, you have to quit praying in English. . . . You simply lapse into silence and resolve to speak not a syllable of any language you have ever learned. Your thoughts are focused on Christ, and then you simply lift up your voice and speak out confidently, in the faith that the Lord will take the sound you give him, and shape it into a language. You take no thought of what you are saying: as far as you are concerned, it is just a series of sounds. The first sounds will sound strange and unnatural to your ear, and they may be halting and inarticulate (have you ever heard a baby learning to talk?).[39]

There are several discrepancies between these instructions and the Biblical accounts of tongue-speaking (Acts 2, 10, 19; I Cor. 12-14). First, if there was actually a prayer meeting on the day of Pentecost (Acts 2:1), there is no indication that the disciples stopped praying in their native languages. Second, there is no indication in

---

[38] Dennis J. Bennett, *When Episcopalians Start Speaking in Tongues* (Medford, Oregon: Christian Retreat Center, n.d.).
[39] Cited by John Miles, "Tongues," *Voice*, XLIV (February, 1965), 6. This is the IFCA publication, not the FGBMFI.

any of the accounts that believers lapsed into silence and resolved to speak in other languages. Third, Paul said to pray with the understanding (I Cor. 14:15). This is in direct conflict to take no thought of what you are saying. Fourth, halting, inarticulate baby talk is contrary to Paul's admonition to put away baby talk (I Cor. 13:11) and to be mature (I Cor. 14:20).

Harold Bredesen gave these instructions to tongue seekers at Yale:

> (1) to think visually and concretely, rather than abstractedly: for example, to try to visualize Jesus as a person; (2) consciously to yield their voices and organs of speech to the Holy Spirit; (3) to repeat certain elementary sounds which he told them, such as "bah—bah—bah," or something similar. He then laid his hands on the head of each seeker, prayed for him, and the seeker did actually speak in tongues.[40]

The instructions to repeat certain elementary sounds were heard personally by the author.[41] Sometimes these instructions to repeat certain words have come through visions.[42] One person had a vision of a ticker tape with unusual words printed on it. His oral repetition of the words caused him to speak in tongues. Another saw a vision of bright lights in the form of letters. Again, there are discrepancies between these instructions and illustrations and the Biblical record. First, there are no indications in the Biblical accounts that persons were "primed" or instructed to repeat certain sounds in order to facilitate the experience. The Holy Spirit gave them utterance (Acts 2:4), not some tongue-teachers or visions. Second, in at least two instances (Acts 2, 10), there was no laying on of the hands at the time of speaking in tongues. Third, in all three Biblical accounts (Acts 2, 10, 19) there is no evidence that one person prayed that another might speak in tongues.

In conclusion, the principle of giving instructions for speaking in tongues is foreign to the Biblical record. Men spoke in tongues spontaneously as the Spirit prompted them. It would appear that no reference was made to tongue-speaking before the person actually did so (Mark 16:17 notwithstanding). In one instance (Acts 10:45), the phenomenon took everyone by surprise.

---

[40] Cited by Stanley D. Walters, "Speaking in Tongues," *Youth in Action* (May, 1964), p. 11.
[41] See Appendix I.
[42] McCandlish Phillips, " 'And There Appeared to Them Tongues of Fire,' " *Saturday Evening Post* (May 16, 1964), p. 31.

Occasion of the Modern Movement

Despite aggressive promotion by the Pentecostal movement in the past fifty years, there was little interest in the phenomenon of speaking in tongues. Why? Because the movement was outside the main denominations; now, it is within. What has occasioned this new awareness and acceptance of the phenomenon? Answers are forthcoming from both those who favor and those who oppose the movement.

The advocates[43] regard the movement as the sovereign work of the Holy Spirit in opposition to widespread wickedness and the promotion of atheistic teachings, both communist and humanist. Second, many Christians are frustrated because of a lack of spiritual power and ability to serve the Lord effectively. Speaking in tongues supplies this power and ability. Third, the strong proclamation of the full gospel (healing, baptism of the Holy Spirit, imminent return of Christ) by Pentecostal ministers has stimulated a hunger in many hearts for a more fervent expression of some of these dynamic truths. Fourth, the increase in mass communications and publicity techniques has projected the full gospel into new denominational areas.

An interested observer, Frederick Schiotz, president of the American Lutheran Church, speculated: "Perhaps it is a reaction against the tendency to over-intellectualize the Christian faith. Speaking seems to fill a spiritual need for simplicity and emotional attachment."[44]

John Miles, an opponent, listed five reasons for the rise of the modern tongues movement.[45] First, there has been a departure from systematic Bible study and particularly the Bible viewed dispensationally. This can be seen in the vehement rejection of the dispensationalist teaching on the ministry of the Holy Spirit in different ages and the transitional nature of the book of Acts. Dispensationalism has often been misrepresented and misunderstood by these people and others. Second, liberal churches are starved for the Word of God and yet want the supernatural. Many tongue-speakers are members of churches that have been bathed in liberalism and neo-orthodoxy. Their churches emphasize the ecumenicity of

[43] "The Neo-Pentecostal Movement," *The Pentecostal Evangel* (May 2, 1965), p. 4.
[44] "Taming the Tongues," *loc. cit.*
[45] John Miles, "Spiritual Gifts and Christian Victory," *Voice*, XLIV (May, 1965),9.

the World Council of Churches and neglect the message of the cross. Third, fundamental churches are often dead. This will prompt many to seek an experience elsewhere. Fourth, some people are looking for an easy way, a spiritual experience that will immediately solve all their problems and frustrations. Fifth, many want a sense experience of the supernatural. They want to walk by sight, rather than by faith and mere adherence to the Word of God. Harry Ironside, who was delivered from the holiness movement, called the tongues movement of his day "disgusting" with "all its attendant delusions and insanities." He concluded: "An unhealthy craving for new and thrilling religious sensations, and emotional meetings of a most exciting character, readily account for these things."[46]

Evaluations of the Modern Movement

Divine? Satanic? Psychological? Artificial? All of these alternatives have been suggested as the proper evaluation of the source or origin of the modern phenomenon of speaking in tongues. Opinions are not necessarily limited to just one alternative; some believe that speaking in tongues can be attributed to two or more of these sources. Edman, chancellor of Wheaton College and a non-speaker in tongues, concluded that modern speaking in tongues could be divine, demonic, or psychological, dependent upon the source.[47] Jack Hayford, National Youth Representative of the International Church of the Foursquare Gospel and a tongues-speaker, admitted that some tongues were satanic, that others were psychologically produced, but that some were a genuine work of God.[48] The fact that the phenomenon of speaking in tongues has taken place is not denied by either side. What is contested is the source of the experience. Since both sides admit that the phenomenon can be caused by one or more sources, this creates no small problem. Who can say what is the source of each particular instance of speaking in tongues? What standard do you use or apply to determine the source of the experience? The experience itself cannot be referred to as the determining factor because it is admitted that the experience can be caused in several ways. There must be an objective, authoritative standard, and there is—the Word of God. This must be the

---

[46] H. A. Ironside, *Holiness, the False and the True* (New York: Loizeaux Brothers, 1947), p. 38.
[47] Edman, *op. cit.*, p. 17.
[48] Jack Hayford, Letter to the Editor, *Christianity Today*, VIII (October 25, 1963), 22.

only and the final authority in determining the actual source of any experience.

Divine

Bredesen saw in the modern tongues movement a definite work of the Holy Spirit:

> During the first half of the Twentieth Century we saw the Holy Spirit breaking down the walls between the Churches, and called it the "ecumenical movement." We saw Him at work alongside the historic churches and called it "the third force." Now, in the second half of the century, we are seeing Him move within the churches. We call it the "charismatic revival."[49]

One would question Bredesen's identification of the ecumenical movement as a work of the Holy Spirit rather than the human activity of certain liberal or neo-orthodox church leaders. If this statement is any gauge to his spiritual and Biblical insight and knowledge, one would have a perfect right to question his evaluation of the charismatic revival. However, Bredesen does not stand alone in his evaluation. Tongue-speakers in both the Pentecostal and the historic, denominational churches would agree with him.

Many others have sounded a warning and an admonition as to the possible divine origin of this movement. They feel that conservatives should not forbid others to speak in tongues (I Cor. 14:39) and that they should follow the advice of Gamaliel: "Refrain from these men, and let them alone: for if this counsel or this work be of men, it will come to nought: But if it be of God, ye cannot overthrow it: lest haply ye be found even to fight against God" (Acts 5:38-39). This seems to be a prevalent opinion among many conservative leaders today who themselves have not spoken in tongues. One typical example is Philip Hughes, a contributing editor of *Christianity Today*, who said:

> Dare we deny that this is a movement of God's sovereign Spirit? Ought we not rather to hope and pray that this may be the beginning of a great spiritual revival within the church in our time? and to rejoice over the zeal and the joy in Christ of those who testify to this experience?[50]

---

[49] *Return to the Charismata* (Van Nuys, Calif.: Blessed Trinity Society, n.d.), tract.

[50] Philip Edgcumbe Hughes, "Review of Christian Religious Thought," *Christianity Today*, VI (May 11, 1962), 63.

In answer to the question, "What is your opinion on speaking in tongues?" Evangelist Billy Graham replied that he had not had the experience but that it was a wonderful experience for those who had.[51] Apparently, Graham accepts the divine source of some of the phenomenon in the world today.

Satanic

Many conservatives believe that speaking in tongues ceased in the apostolic era and that any manifestation of the phenomenon since that time must be regarded as not only a simulated counterfeit, but actually of Satanic origin.[52] Under Satanic influence, the magicians of Egypt were able to duplicate the divine miracles performed by Moses (Ex. 7:10—8:7). In the Great Tribulation, the anti-Christ will be able to duplicate the miracles of Jesus Christ with Satanic power (II Thess. 2:9). Christ even predicted that miracles and prophesying would be done in His name apart from His sanction or power (Matt. 7:21-23). Apparently professing Christians can do great things, even bring glory to Christ, but yet still do it in the power of Satan. This is why an experience or miracle, no matter how great, cannot be appealed to as the sole judge of the source of that event. For this reason, many feel that speaking in tongues can be done by professing Christians in a Christian atmosphere and for the glory of Christ, and yet still have its origin in Satan.

Stegall believed that there was a distinct connection between the sources of behavior in tongue-speakers and spiritualist mediums.[53] The visible, physical effects (shaking of arms and body) caused by the supernatural control were the same. The person's breathing and stance were affected in the same way. The description of what it feels like to be under the power (e.g., current of electricity passing through the body) was the same.

Both the advocates and the opponents of speaking in tongues admit that demon possession and/or influence can be the cause of supernatural utterances in the lives of believers. Edman wrote: "To the uninstructed Christian insistent upon having some particular

---

[51] Heard on the radio program, "Conversation Piece," WHIO, Dayton, Ohio, November 16, 1964.

[52] Herman A. Hoyt, "Speaking in Tongues," *Brethren Missionary Herald*, XXV (April 20, 1963), 206. Also, I. M. Haldeman, *Holy Ghost Baptism and Speaking with Tongues.*

[53] Stegall, *op. cit.*, pp. 48-49. Comparisons are shown by statements made by both groups.

gift of the Spirit, and thus ignoring the sovereignty of the Holy Spirit, there can be the dreadful reality of the gift of tongues by demonic power. I have known such in my experience."[54] Raymond Frame, a former missionary to China, had this experience and agreed:

> Evil spirits can easily find opportunity to operate in the believer's emotional life—especially when the believer is persuaded to suspend all intellectual activity and to yield his will over to an invisible intelligence (whom the Christian, of course, is persuaded to regard as being the Holy Spirit Himself). For this reason the child of God who becomes preoccupied with that least of all gifts, tongues, places himself in a particularly vulnerable position in relation to the danger of demon depression, obsession, or actual possession.[55]

Thus, Satanic power must be regarded as a live option as to the source of the modern tongues phenomenon.

Psychological

The humanistic, secularistic world which denies the existence of the supernatural, whether it be divine or demonic, would classify all experiences of speaking in tongues as psychological or physiological in character and in source.

Some conservative Christians also describe the character of modern, genuine glossolalia as psychological. Bergsma, a Christian psychiatrist, related the phenomenon to the science of cybernetics which deals with the storage and the recall of memory. He wrote:

> Obviously nothing can come out of each individual brain that was not once previously stored there. Materials stored may be altered, fragmented, confused, distorted but cannot be humanly created. Also, it is obvious that language . . . which comes out as language in glossolalia, must have been introduced somehow in that person's life. Even if that person was not conscious he or she had heard those words, or that a memory engram was being recorded, these had nevertheless been previously deposited there. *This will explain the very few cases of modern glossolalia, if there are any.*[56] (Italics, mine.)

This evaluation sounds plausible, but it is not without problems. This position must assume that modern genuine glossolalia is not prompted by God and is not of equal character to Biblical tongue-speaking. If

[54] Edman, *op. cit.*, p. 16.
[55] Raymond Frame, "Something Unusual," *His*, XXIV (December, 1963), 26. Frame exposed himself to this situation. See Appendix III for his description of the experience.
[56] Stuart Bergsma, "Speaking With Tongues," *Torch and Trumpet*, XIV (November, 1964), 10.

it were, then could the Biblical accounts of speaking in tongues be explained by cybernetics or did the Holy Spirit cause the disciples to speak languages which they had never learned or heard? Because of lack of information, this cannot be proved either way. Tongue advocates argue that Bergsma has assumed his conclusion before he has proved it.

Martin, professor of Bible at Berea College, likewise believed that the modern phenomenon was not an evidence of true Holy Spirit possession, but rather "an extreme type of exhibitionism like 'weeping for joy' or hysterical laughter in the midst of mourning. It is simply an emotional and preconceptual outburst of joy."[57] He ascribed it to partially developed catalepsy, hysteria, hypnosis, ecstasy, and psychic catharsis.

Morton Kelsey, an Episcopalian rector and student of the Jungian Psychology (contact with the realm of psychic reality and the entities in it is possible), called speaking in tongues a valid religious experience. He stated: "It is one entrance into the spiritual realm; by giving access to the unconscious, it is one contact with non-physical reality which allows God to speak directly to man."[58] One objection to Kelsey's opinion is apparent. Does God speak directly to men apart from the Word of God? This sounds suspiciously like a statement of neo-orthodoxy. However, the psychological evaluation may explain some of the phenomenon.

Artificial

Another possible explanation for some of the modern phenomenon of speaking in tongues is that it has been artificially produced by the person himself. The person may have desired to have a genuine spiritual experience with the Lord but in actuality did not have it. In the intense emotional atmosphere of the service and the altar call he may try to do what others are doing or what he is told he should do. He may go forward, fall on his knees, raise his hands, and utter strange sounds. Observers may be satisfied that he has manifested the evidence of the baptism of the Holy Spirit and may tell him so.[59] Since he desired this experience, he may accept their opinion that he has done so. In other cases, a person may have

[57] Martin, *op. cit.*, p. 60.
[58] Kelsey, *op. cit.*, p. 231.
[59] The author observed this. See Appendix I.

had a genuine experience with the Lord (confession of sin, dedication of life, etc.), but the climax or physical evidence of the experience may have been artificial. Accepting the authoritative instructions of the pastor or counsellor as the directive will of God, he may do exactly what they say and go through the motions. After all, he does not want them to think that he does not want the Lord's best for his life. He may repeat the elementary sounds (which are suggested to him) and others believing that this is the way speaking in tongues is done. There are still others who know that speaking in tongues is a status symbol of spiritual achievement in their assemblies and therefore simulate the experience in order to gain religious stature and praise from others. Such artificial simulation of religious experiences is not peculiar to Pentecostal tongues services. In many conservative, traditional church meetings, people have gone forward at the altar call just because their friends did so or because staying in the pew would be too conspicuous. Since gibberish or ecstatic speech is accepted as a form of tongue-speaking (other than foreign languages) it would be very easy to simulate such repetitive sounds whenever necessary. Walters found such an example in the so-called Yale outburst of tongues:

> Of the students involved, some later became unsure that the outbreak was a genuine work of the Spirit. I talked to one who had spoken in tongues when Mr. Bredesen first visited the campus, could do so later whenever he wished, and on his own initiative *did so in my presence*, yet doubted that it was a work of the Spirit. A devout Christian, he was genuinely perplexed.[60]

Thus, the artificial simulation of the phenomenon of speaking in tongues must be regarded as a definite possibility for many of the cases.

Summary

Four possible opinions as to the source of modern glossolalia have been presented. Both sides admit that the phenomenon can be satanically, psychologically, and artificially produced. However, the advocates believe that much tongue-speaking has been produced by God. The author believes that the origin of modern speaking in tongues cannot be limited to just one source, but that all modern glossolalia *can* be explained by the first three mentioned. That

---

[60] Walters, *op. cit.*, p. 10.

modern glossolalia is not divinely produced at all will be demonstrated in the following chapters. It simply is not in accord with the written Word of God, the only and the final authority in faith and practice.

Conclusion

The nature of the modern tongues movement is complex. It is composed of both saved and unsaved, of both Calvinists and Arminians, and of members of both Pentecostal and non-Pentecostal churches and denominations.

The Full Gospel Business Men's Fellowship International and the Blessed Trinity Society are spearheading the movement. They are attempting to achieve their goals through private prayer groups, banquets, conventions, and publications. Key periodicals which are actively promoting the movement are *Voice, View, Vision, Trinity,* and *Christian Life.* Key glossolalia personalities are Demos Shakarian, Oral Roberts, David du Plessis, Harold Bredesen, Jean Stone, and Dennis Bennett.

The modern tongues movement has had a wide outreach. The secular world has manifested an interest in the phenomenon through radio, television, and printed articles. Both liberal and conservative schools and missionary agencies have been penetrated. Practically all of the major historic denominations now have tongue-speakers within their ranks, both among the clergy and the laity. Well-known secular and sacred personalities have testified to the presence of the phenomenon in their lives.

The characteristics of the modern tongues movement are somewhat different from those of the old Pentecostalism, and yet in many ways similar. Tongue adherents are found in both the professional and the working classes and in all the cultural, economic strata. Speaking in tongues is not manifested alone. It is accompanied, preceded and followed by such phenomena as the sound of wind, fire, perfume fragrance, physical convulsions, electirc shocks, lights, perspiration, healings, and visions, including seeing, hearing, and touching Christ. Tongue-speakers have testified to changed lives as the result of their experiences. The modern phenomenon does not frequently occur spontaneously; instructions are given as to the mechanics of speaking in tongues. It is encouraged and prompted by men.

The occasion of the modern movement is controversial, dependent upon one's perspective. Advocates feel that it is the divine reaction and answer to the wickedness of the world, the weakness of Christians, and the coldness of the churches. Opponents believe that it is the result of a dearth of Bible study and genuine Christian experience; therefore many are looking for an acceptable substitute and an antidote for their spiritual lethargy.

The evaluations of the modern tongues movement are many. It has been classified as divinely produced, counterfeited by Satan, psychologically caused, or artificially simulated. Advocates admit all four possibilities, but emphasize the first. Opponents would limit the sources of the modern phenomenon to the last three.

CHAPTER IV

THE LANGUAGE OF SPEAKING IN TONGUES

When people spoke in tongues in New Testament times, did they speak in known foreign languages, unknown ecstatic speech, or in both kinds? Do modern tongue-speakers speak in known foreign languages, unknown ecstatic speech, or in both kinds? Do the two groups correspond? An investigation into the nature of the language or speech spoken is necessary to an understanding of the phenomenon itself and to a proper evaluation of the modern tongues movement.

Various Views

Expository Comments

A contemporary liberal writer believed that foreign languages or ecstatic speech were not involved in the Biblical phrase "speaking in tongues." He related it to decisive expository preaching. He translated *glossai* (tongues or languages) as "pericopes," chosen passages of Scripture with or without comments, which formed a usual part of the public worship service. These Scriptures and expository comments became fixed by tradition, and were read or recited on certain holy days. Why then were the multitudes amazed at what the disciples said (Acts 2:6)? Sirks replied: "But they are not the pericopes expected on this feast-day; they are different from those prescribed by tradition. . . . but the radical change is that the disciples either chose pericopes other than the familiar ones, or interpreted them differently. . . . the pericopes were expounded in such a way as to point to Jesus."[1] According to Sirks, the multitudes were not amazed at the *vehicle* of speech, but rather the *content* of the speech. They had never heard these Scriptures recited during the feast of Pentecost before nor had they ever heard them exegetically applied to Jesus. Sirks also cited the experience of Jesus in the

[1] G. J. Sirks, "The Cinderella of Theology: The Doctrine of the Holy Spirit, *Harvard Theological Review*, L (April, 1957), 86.

synagogue at Nazareth (Luke 4:16-30) as an illustration of deliberate deviation from the prescribed pericopes of the worship service.

This is an extreme view and would be rejected by most liberals and by all conservatives. It must be regarded as a naturalistic attempt to explain away a supernatural phenomenon. No doubt the multitudes were amazed at the content of the tongues phenomenon and of Peter's subsequent sermon, but this should not detract from their confusion over the fact that the disciples were speaking in other languages or dialects which they had not learned (Acts 2:4,6-8,11). Also, the equation of "tongues" with "pericopes" cannot explain the other appearances of the Biblical phenomenon which did not always occur during Jewish feasts or worship services.

Ecstatic Speech

There are a few writers who believe that every instance of the Biblical phenomenon of speaking in tongues was in the form of ecstatic speech. Gilmour, a liberal theologian from the Andover Newton Theological School, said that "early Christian glossolalia was the utterance of gibberish at the compulsion of ecstatic and uncontrolled emotion—a cacophony unintelligible to all save the few who were charismatically endowed for its interpretation."[2] Again, this is a liberal attempt to explain away the supernatural source of a Biblical phenomenon in the terms of human, ecstatic, uncontrolled emotion. His evolutionary concept of the development of religion would cause him to conclude that Christianity has advanced beyond this primitive and crude expression of worship.

Others believe that all Biblical tongue-speaking was in the form of ecstatic speech, but for different reasons. How then do they explain the apparent fact that the multitudes heard foreign languages being spoken (Acts 2:6,8,11)? Barclay said that Luke had confused speaking with tongues with *foreign* tongues.[3] This conclusion stems from the higher critical views of the denial of Biblical inspiration and of the belief in the human errancy of the autographa. As such, it must be rejected. Some conservatives believe that the disciples either spoke in their native tongue or in ecstatic

[2] S. MacLean Gilmour, "Easter and Pentecost," *Journal of Biblical Literature*, LXXXI (March, 1962), p. 64.
[3] William Barclay, *The Acts of the Apostles* (Philadelphia: The Westminster Press, 1955), p. 16.

speech.[4] They further state that the Holy Spirit caused the foreign listeners to hear the speech in their foreign, native tongues. If the disciples spoke in their native tongue, then the Biblical phenomenon was strictly a miracle of hearing. If the disciples spoke in ecstatic speech, then the miracle was twofold—both in the speaking and the hearing. However, it is difficult to reconcile these assertions with the clear statement that the disciples began to speak with other tongues before the multitude arrived (Acts 2:4) and with the equation of "tongues" and "dialects" (Acts 2:4; cf. 2:6).

Foreign Languages

One prevalent opinion is that all Biblical instances of speaking in tongues was in the form of foreign languages. This position was and is held by both non-tongue speakers (Barnes, Henry, Ironside, Lange, Lenski, Rice) and possibly by a few tongue-speakers. The following statement by Horton, a tongues advocate, is somewhat ambiguous as to the nature of the languages spoken, but it may refer just to foreign languages:

> Then there is a notion abroad that tongues are a kind of gibberish, incoherent and non-intelligible, a series of uninterpretable glossal noises. No. Tongues were and are languages. They are mostly unknown to the hearers and always to the speakers. But they might on occasion be known to the hearers, as at Pentecost, where the tongues were unknown as they were spoken and known as they were heard.[5]

Even if this statement refers to languages other than known, foreign languages, it shows that some Pentecostals are opposed to gibberish or mere repetition of certain sounds as the basic nature of speaking in tongues (and this latter form of speaking is taking place today).

The supporting proofs for the view of foreign languages will be presented later in the chapter.

Ecstatic Speech and Foreign Languages

The most dominant opinion among both tongue-speakers and non-tongue speakers is that the Biblical phenomenon of speaking in tongues could consist of either ecstatic speech or foreign languages. Usually, foreign languages are identified with the phenomenon in

---

[4] Richard Belward Rackham, *The Acts of the Apostles* (London: Methuen & Co., Ltd., 1953), p. 19.
[5] Harold Horton, *The Gifts of the Spirit* (Bedfordshire, England: Redemption Tidings Bookroom, 1946), pp. 159-60.

Acts and ecstatic speech with that in First Corinthians. Charles Ryrie, dean of the Graduate School of Dallas Theological Seminary, is typical of non-tongue speakers in his definition of the gift of tongues: "This was a God-given ability to speak in another language, either in a foreign, human language or an unknown ecstatic utterance."[6] Harold Bredesen, a director of the Blessed Trinity Society and a tongues-speaker, claimed to have witnessed to foreigners in their own languages, but unknown to him (such as Polish and Coptic Egyptian); however, he stated that most of the current glossolalia is in the form of unknown languages.[7] A discussion of the pro and con arguments of this position will be presented later in this chapter.

New Testament Meaning

Basic to any discipline is a study of words with their meanings and usages. This is especially important in dealing with the Biblical phenomenon of speaking in tongues. The key word of this phenomenon is *glossa*, translated consistently as "tongue" in the A.V. When the meaning and the usage of this term have been determined, then a proper evaluation of the modern tongues movement will be able to be set forth.

Occurrences

The Greek word *glossa* occurs fifty times in the New Testament with various usages. It is used fifteen times of the organ of the physical body which is used in speaking (Mark 7:33,35; Luke 1:64; Acts 2:26; Rom. 3:13; 14:11; I Cor. 14:9; Phil. 2:11; James 1:26; 3:5,6 [twice], 8; I Peter 3:10; Rev. 16:10). It is used once of the tongue of the intermediate body, the body which a person has between death and resurrection (Luke 16:24). It is used once figuratively of "cloven tongues like as of fire" (Acts 2:3). It is used once of the word content of speaking in contrast to a deed of action (I John 3:18; or perhaps this is another reference to the physical organ). In the book of Revelation, it is used seven times in connection with kindred, people, nations, and multitudes to describe ethnic groups that are characterized by speaking certain foreign languages (5:9; 7:9;

---

[6] Charles Caldwell Ryrie, *Biblical Theology of the New Testament* (Chicago: Moody Press, 1959), p. 194.
[7] Cited by Farrell, *op. cit.*, p. 6.

10:11; 11:9; 13:7; 14:6; 17:5). The word is used twenty-five times to describe the actual phenomenon of speaking in tongues (Mark 16:17; Acts 2:4-11; 10:46; 19:6; I Cor. 12:10 [twice], 28,30; 13: 1,8; 14:2,4,5 [twice], 6,13,14,18,19,22,23,26,27,29). Thus the Biblical writers used this one word to denote at least five or six ideas; and yet, these usages are all inter-related, with one possible exception (figurative usage of Acts 2). They all deal with the basic entity of speech, either the organ of speaking or the act, the content, the language, and the results of speaking.

Phrases

There is no set pattern by which *glossa* is used to describe the phenomenon of speaking in tongues. It appears in nine different constructions. Once it is described as "new tongues" (*glossais . . . kainais*; Mark 16:17). It is also called "other tongues" (*heterais glossais*; Acts 2:4). It appears once as a plural noun with the definite article (*hai glossai*; I Cor. 14:22) and twice as a plural noun without the definite article (I Cor. 12:10; 13:8). It is used with *gene* to indicate "kinds of tongues" (*gene glosson*; I Cor. 12:10) or "diversities of tongues" (I Cor. 12:28). Most often it is used in the dative plural along with the verb *laleo,* "to speak" (Mark 16:17; Acts 2:4,11; 10:46; 19:6; I Cor. 12:30; 13:1; 14:5 [twice], 6,18, 23,39). It is also used in the dative singular with the verb *laleo* (I Cor. 14:2,4,13,19,27). Once it is used with the verb "to pray" (*proseuchomai glossei*; I Cor. 14:14) and once with the verb "to have" (*echei glossan*; I Cor. 14:26).

Lexical Meanings

Abbott-Smith defined *glossa* as the organ of speech, a language, and as "unintelligible sounds uttered in spiritual ecstacy."[8]

Thayer denoted *glossa* as the member of the body, the organ of speech, and as a language used by a particular people in distinction from that of other nations. He further added that it was "the gift of men who, rapt in an ecstasy and no longer quite masters of their own reason and consciousness, pour forth their glowing spiritual emotions in strange utterances, rugged, dark, disconnected, quite unfitted to instruct or to influence the minds of others."[9]

[8] G. Abbott-Smith, *A Manual Greek Lexicon of the New Testament* (Edinburgh: T. & T. Clark, 1954), p. 93.

[9] Joseph Henry Thayer, *A Greek-English Lexicon of the New Testament* (Edinburgh: T. & T. Clark, 1953), p. 118.

Arndt and Gingrich classified *glossa* in three ways. First, it can be used literally as the organ of speech or figuratively of forked flames. Second, it was used of foreign languages and as a synonym for tribe, people, or nation. Third, it referred to the broken speech of persons in religious ecstasy. This could be either antiquated, foreign, unintelligible, mysterious utterances or marvelous, heavenly languages.[10]

Kittel likewise followed the other lexicographers and defined *glossa* as the organ of speech, language, or glossolalia which is an unintelligible, ecstatic utterance. He claimed that one of its forms of expression is a muttering of words or sounds without interconnection or meaning. He identified this ecstatic speech with the language which is used in heaven between God and the angels and to which men may attain in prayer as they are seized by the Spirit and caught up into heaven.[11]

Moulton and Milligan, from a study of the Greek papyri, added that the word is used not only for language, but also for local peculiarities of speech.[12]

This survey of lexical meanings has shown that linguistic scholars regard the phenomenon of glossolalia as being both foreign languages and ecstatic utterances, with primary emphasis and application on the latter.

New Testament Usage

The meanings of Biblical terms must always be determined by the usage of those terms. As valuable as lexical meanings and word derivations are, they must always be subordinated to the usage by the Biblical writers. A study of the New Testament usage of *glossa* will reveal the fact that when used of the phenomenon of speaking in tongues it always refers to foreign languages. It cannot refer to both foreign languages and unknown ecstatic utterances as the modern tongues advocates claim. The following proofs from the relevant Biblical passages should support this conclusion.

The very choice of *glossa* to describe the phenomenon is significant. Under the section on occurrences, it was shown that the

---

[10] William F. Arndt and F. Wilbur Gingrich, *A Greek-English Lexicon of the New Testament* (Chicago: The University of Chicago Press, 1957), p. 161.
[11] Kittel, *op. cit.*, pp. 721-26.
[12] James Hope Moulton and George Milligan, *The Vocabulary of the Greek New Testament* (Grand Rapids: Wm. B. Eerdmans Publishing Company, 1963), p. 128.

word was used of the physical organ which gave forth audible, known sounds of various human languages. Even the organ of the intermediate body (Luke 16:24) spoke intelligible language, known to the listeners. It could be used as a denotation for an ethnic group (Rev. 5:9; 7:9) because nations or peoples are distinguised by the languages which they speak. These are Russian because they speak only Russian; these are Japanese because they speak only Japanese. In several occurrences of speaking in tongues (Acts 2:4,6,8,11; 10:46; 19:6) only foreign languages were spoken. Meanings in obscure passages must always be determined by meanings in clear passages. The very fact that *glossa* is used over and over to designate the organ of, the content of, and the groups denoted by known languages should be a strong determinative factor in fixing the meaning of the term when used of the phenomenon of speaking in tongues.

In Mark's textually disputed passage (Mark 16:9-20), it is predicted that believers would "speak with new tongues" (*glossais lalesousin kainais*; 16:17). Assuming that the passage is genuine, the usage of the adjective *kainos* rather than its synonym *neos* is noteworthy. According to Abbott-Smith, *kainos* refers to "the new primarily in reference to quality, the fresh, unworn" whereas *neos* refers to the recent."[13] It is admitted by all that the phenomenon of speaking in tongues did not occur in the Old Testament or Gospel periods and that it first happened on the day of Pentecost (Acts 2). Therefore, if speaking in tongues had involved unknown languages never spoken before, Christ would have used *neos* (new in time). But since He used *kainos*, this must refer to foreign languages which were new to the speaker, but which had been in existence before. Arguments based upon word synonyms are sometimes hard to maintain, but there must be a good reason why *kainos*, not *neos*, was used. The fact that the disciples did speak in known, foreign languages on the day of Pentecost (Acts 2:4,6,8,11) would support this distinction and conclusion.

When the Holy Spirit filled the disciples on the day of Pentecost, they "began to speak with other tongues (*lalein heterais glossais*), as the Spirit gave them utterance" (Acts 2:4). What are these other tongues"? Were they unknown or foreign languages? Luke has

---

[13] Abbott-Smith, *op. cit.*, p. 226.

defined them in the very words of the listeners. The multitude was confounded "because that every man heard them speak in his own language" (*tei idia dialekto*; 1:6). The multitude questioned: "And how hear we every man in our own tongue, wherein we were born?" (*tei idia dialekto*; 2:8). Later, they said: " . . . we do hear them speak in our tongues (*tais hemeterais glossais*) the wonderful works of God" (2:11). The multitude could understand the content of the phenomenon because the disciples were speaking in their own dialects and languages. These were definitely foreign languages being spoken. What languages were they? Luke classified them as "Parthians, and Medes, and Elamites, and the dwellers in Mesopotamia, and in Judaea, and Cappadocia, in Pontus, and Asia, Phrygia, and Pamphylia, in Egypt, and in the parts of Libya about Cyrene, and strangers of Rome, Jews and proselytes, Cretes and Arabians" (2:9-11). Not only did the disciples speak different languages, but they also spoke various dialects of the same language. "The Phrygians and Pamphylians, for instance, both spoke Greek, but in different idioms; the Parthians, Medes, and Elamites all spoke Persian, but in different provincial forms."[14] Why did Luke include such a long list of countries and peoples? He wanted to make it clear that the disciples spoke in foreign languages and dialects, not in unknown sounds. This first instance of the phenomenon of speaking in tongues sets the Biblical pattern and standard for all subsequent tongue-speaking. It must be in foreign languages, and it must be the foreign languages of those who are present when the gift of interpretation is not exercised.

The second clear instance of speaking in tongues took place in the experience of Cornelius and his household (Acts 10:44-48). The evidence that they had believed in Christ and had received the Holy Spirit was the phenomenon of speaking in tongues: "For they heard them speak with tongues (*lalounton glossais*), and magnify God" (10:46). That this speaking was in foreign languages is quite apparent. First, Luke used the same words here to describe the phenomenon as he did in the earlier account (2:4,11). The natural impression left with the reader is that the same phenomenon has taken place. Foreign languages and/or dialects have been spoken. Second, how could the listeners know that Cornelius and his house-

[14] Marvin R. Vincent, *Word Studies in the New Testament* (New York: Charles Scribner's Sons, 1908), I, 450.

hold were magnifying God unless they could understand them? This argument naturally assumes that magnifying God was part or all of the substance of this phenomenon. Third, in Peter's subsequent report to the Jerusalem church, he said that the Gentiles had received the "like gift" (11:17) and that "the Holy Ghost fell on them as on us at the beginning" (11:15). This undoubtedly refers to the experience of Pentecost. This likeness of experience extends not only to the fact of receiving the Spirit but to the nature of tongue-speaking in foreign languages.

The third and final instance of speaking in tongues in Acts is found in the experience of the twelve disciples of John the Baptist at Ephesus (19:1-7). When the Holy Spirit came upon them, "they spake with tongues (*elaloun te glossais*) and prophesied" (19:6). Since Luke again uses the same basic words to describe the phenomenon as in the earlier two cases, it is logical to infer that the same experience took place and that this speaking was also in foreign languages. Also, if prophecy was a part of this tongues phenomenon, then Paul must have understood what they were speaking in tongues.

Many advocates of modern tongue-speaking will admit that speaking in foreign languages constituted the phenomenon in the book of Acts, but they will argue that the gift of tongues (I Cor. 12-14) will permit speaking in both unknown and foreign languages. However, a study of this Pauline letter will reveal that the nature of the phenomenon in the two books is the same (speaking in foreign languages), although the purposes may be different.

When Paul introduced the subject of spiritual gifts, he stated that "no man speaking by the Spirit of God called Jesus accursed (ANATHEMA JESUS): and that no man can say that Jesus is the Lord, but by the Holy Ghost" (I Cor. 12:3). Could it be that some Corinthian in a human effort to reproduce the gift of speaking in tongues rearranged and pronounced certain syllables with the total effect of actually calling Jesus accursed? There is a striking similarity between "accursed" (*anathema*) and "our Lord cometh" *marana tha*) in certain sounds (I Cor. 16:22). A Greek speaker may have tried to simulate this latter Aramaic phrase with the faulty re-arrangement of *a-na-tha-mar*. Thus, he would have been calling Jesus accursed rather than declaring His coming. Another possibility is that the person said "Jesus is accursed" (*anathema*) instead of "Jesus is a votive offering" (*anatheima*) or that he substituted "accursed" for "a curse" (*katara*; cf. Gal. 3:13). Whatever the case might have been, the person was attempting to simulate syllables of a known language, not an unknown one. Whatever he said was also in the vocabulary of a known language. This must be considered as a plausible interpretation because this verse is found within the context of spiritual gifts.

Paul designated the gift of tongues as *gene glosson*, translated as "kinds of tongues" (I Cor. 12:10) and "diversities of tongues" (I Cor. 12:28). This term *genos* refers to a family, offspring, race, nation, kind, sort, and class in New Testament usage. It always depicts that which is related to each other. There are many "kinds" of fish (Matt. 13:47), but they are all fish. There are several "kinds" of demons in the world (Matt. 17:21), but they are all still demons. There are many "kinds" of voices (I Cor. 14:10), but they are all voices. From this it can be concluded that there are many "kinds" of languages, but they are all languages. There are several families of languages in the world—Semitic, Slavic, Latin, etc. These are all related in that they have a definite vocabulary and grammatical construction. Paul coud not have possibly combined known, foreign languages with unknown, ecstatic utterances under the same classification. They simply are not related to each other.

Always connected with the gift of tongues is the gift of intrepretation of tongues (*hermeneia glosson*; I Cor. 12:10; 14:26,28). What does "interpret" mean? In non-charismatic passages, it refers to an exposition of Old Testament Scripture (Luke 24:27) or to a translation from one known, foreign language to another (John 1:39,43; 9:7; Heb. 7:2). In both cases, it is an attempt to make clear through explanation or translation what is said in a known language. These usages must govern the meaning of the gift of interpretation. Interpretation of speaking in tongues (foreign languages) was necessary in order to make clear what was said to the listeners. This was done through translation into the common language and/or exposition.

The statement, "Though I speak with the tongues of men and of angels" (*ean tais glossais ton anthropon lalo kai ton angelon*; I Cor. 13:1), has caused some to divide the tongues phenomenon into known languages ("of men") and unknown languages ("of angels"). However, this is not necessarily so. First, Paul was describing a hypothetical case ("if"; *ean*). This does not mean that he had spoken in angelic languages even though he later admitted that he did speak in tongues (I Cor. 14:18). Second, the very fact that the word "tongues" is used just once with "men" and "angels" shows that human and angelic languages can be grouped together. They have something in common. They are both languages, known and understood by the listeners. Third, whenever men and angels conversed together in Biblical times, they were able to carry on an intelligent conversation in known languages without difficulty or interpretation. Rather than dividing languages into known and unknown, Paul is affirming that all tongues phenomena were in the form of definite languages, not ecstatic utterances.

The insertion of the adjective "unknown" (I Cor. 14:2,4,13, 14,19,27) into the Authorized Version by the translators was most unfortunate. In the English text, it appears in italics, which in this instance means that the word is not found in the original Greek text. The translators added this explanatory word because they thought that the Corinthian tongues phenomenon consisted of speaking in an unknown, ecstatic utterance. The presence of "unknown" just conveys the wrong impression and should not be used as an argument for the view of ecstatic, unknown utterances or languages.

Some believe that the phrase "no man understandeth him" (I Cor. 14:2) is a categorical statement. This means that if a representative from every known language group were present at a tongues meeting, no one would be able to recognize or to understand what was being spoken by the person who was speaking in tongues. However, to be consistent then, the advocates of tongue-speaking would have to say that every occurrence of tongue-speaking must be in the form of unknown languages, and yet, they admit that many of their own group have spoken in known foreign languages. Thus, this would constitute an argument against their position that both known and unknown languages can be spoken. Actually, this verse only means that no man *present at the service* understands the speaker. Since God was the source of genuine glossolalia, He knew what language groups were present and caused the person to speak in a foreign language not represented. Thus, the gift of interpretation was always necessary.

As an illustration of proper tongue-speaking, Paul wrote: "And even things without life giving sound, whether pipe or harp, *except they give a distinction in the sounds,* how shall it be known what is piped or harped?" (I Cor. 14:7). As musical sounds are distinguished by various notes of the scale and octave, so speaking is distinguished by vocabulary and grammatical construction. Paul was opposed to the mere repetition of certain sounds or "words" (as many modern tongue-speakers do) as the proper expression of the phenomenon of speaking in tongues. Words "easy to be understood" (I Cor. 14:9) should be spoken. A person should be able to recognize the utterance as a known language and thus capable of translation and explanation (I Cor. 14:11).

In dealing with the purpose of tongues, Paul quoted a prophecy from Isaiah (28:11-12): "In the law it is written, with men of other tongues and other lips will I speak unto this people; and yet for all that will they not hear me, saith the Lord" (I Cor. 14:21). This prophecy dealt with the time when Israel and Judah were invaded by the Assyrians (cf. II Kings 17-18). The phrase "this people" refers to the Jews and the phrase "men of other tongues and other lips" refers to the Assyrians. The threats of the Assyrians who spoke both Assyrian and Hebrew did not change the sinfulness and unbelief of the Jews. This speaking in foreign languages was to be a sign to the Jews, but they did not receive it. Paul then applied this truth to the Corinthian situation: "Wherefore tongues are for a sign, not to them that believe, but to them that believe not . . ." (I Cor. 14:22). Since foreign languages are definiely referred to in verse 21 (*heteroglossais*; cf. Acts 2:4, where other tongues are also definitely foreign languages and dialects), then the usage of "tongues" (*hai glossai*) in verse 22 must also refer to foreign languages. This is further confirmed by the usage of the article of previous reference (*hai*) and the function of the inferential conjunction "wherefore" (*hoste*). If Paul considered speaking in tongues to be in an unknown utterance, he would not have used the same word twice in these two verses, especially since the meaning of *glossa* was clearly established in the first usage.

Luke, the associate of Paul, wrote Acts (A.D. 60) after First Corinthians was written (A.D. 55). Luke was undoubtedly acquainted with the contents of First Corinthians either through reading the letter or listening to Paul's teaching. These facts are significant because Luke used the same terms (*glossa* and *laleo*) to describe the phenomenon of speaking in tongues at Jerusalem, Caeserea, and

Ephesus (Acts 2, 10, 19) as Paul did in writing to the Corinthians. Since foreign languages definitely constitute the phenomenon in Acts, then foreign languages must have been spoken at Corinth. If this is not so, then why did not Luke use different phraseology or qualifying words to indicate the difference? Lenski wrote: ". . . Luke is the one who fully describes what the tongues are while Paul takes for granted that his readers know what they are and therefore offers not description."[15] This is very plausible. Theophilus, the recipient of Acts, would need an explanation of this phenomenon, but the Corinthians would not. Hodge added: "If the meaning of the phrase [*glossais*] is thus historically and philologically determined for Acts and Mark, it must also be determined for the Epistle to the Corinthians."[16] Whenever and wherever the phenomenon took place, one would expect its basic nature (speaking in known languages) would be the same.

Speaking in foreign languages which were not learned would certainly constitute a divine miracle; however, speaking in gibberish or in unknown sounds could easily be done by either a Christian or an unsaved person. There is no objective standard by which such speaking could be evaluated. Therefore, it is logical to assume that God would institute a miracle that men could not duplicate through human simulation.

Also, in all cases of conversation and revelation between natural (men) and supernatural beings (God, angels, Satan, demons), the communication was in understandable language. On this basis of precedent and illustration, again it would be logical to assume that speaking in tongues would manifest itself in known, understandable languages.

Before Pentecost, there was one other miracle that involved language and speech. God changed the single speech and the one language of the world into many languages, speech groups at Babel (Gen. 11:1-9). This was a change into foreign languages, not into unknown sounds. Since God performed this type of miracle before, it would be reasonable to believe that He repeated its basic nature at Pentecost.

Arguments, both Scriptural and logical, have been presented

[15] R. C. H. Lenski, *The Interpretation of St. Paul's First and Second Epistle to the Corinthians* (Columbus, Ohio: Wartburg Press, 1957), p. 505.
[16] Charles Hodge, *An Exposition of the First Epistle to the Corinthians* (Grand Rapids: Wm. B. Eerdmans Publishing Co., 1950), p. 248.

to show that the phenomenon of speaking in tongues was done only in known, foreign languages. The burden of proof is upon the modern tongues-speaker to show that Biblical glossolalia also included unknown, ecstatic sounds.

Linguistic Evaluations

To be a renewal or revival of the Biblical spiritual gifts, the modern tongues movement must demonstrate that all tongue-speaking is done in known languages of the world. However, this is not the case. Bredesen admitted that "most of the current glossolalia is unknown languages."[17] The many testimonies of other tongue-speakers would confirm Bredesen's conviction, although a few have claimed to have spoken in known languages.

The conclusions of linguistic scholars have also shown that modern glossolalia consists of unknown sounds and that some of the claims of speaking known languages are false. True glossolalia (speaking a language not previously spoken) is rare. "Mosiman studied many such supposed cases and found not one to be authentic. Robert L. Dean, a contemporaray psychologist, comes to the same conclusion."[18]

William Welmes, professor of African Languages at UCLA, called the modern phenomenon a linguistic fraud and monstrosity. He gave this report on his investigation:

> And I must report without reservation that my sample does *not* sound like a language structurally. There can be no more than two contrasting vowel sounds, and a most peculiarly restricted set of consonant sounds; these combine into a very few syllable clusters which recur many times in various orders. The consonants and vowels do not all sound like English (the glossolalic's native language), but the intonation patterns are so completely American English that the total effect is a bit ludicrous.[19]

Welmes also criticized Bredesen's claim of having spoken in Coptic Egyptian. He said: "The latter must have been in a spiritualist seance, because there have been no native speakers of Coptic Egyptian for a good many years. I fear this is typical of the mistaken, though perhaps sincere, claims of modern glossolalics."[20]

---

[17] Farrell, *op. cit.*, p. 6.
[18] Bergsma, *op. cit.*, p. 9.
[19] William Welmes, Letter to the Editor, *Christianity Today*, VIII (November 8, 1963), 19-20.
[20] *Ibid.*

Eugene Nida, famous linguist of the American Bible Society, came to the following conclusion after his investigation:

> The types of inventory and distributions would indicate clearly that this recording bears no resemblance to any actual language which has ever been treated by linguists. . . . If then, it is not a human language, what is it? One can only say that it is a form of "ecstatic speech." . . . On the basis of what I have learned about this type of phenomena of "tongues" in other parts of the world, apparently there is the same tendency to employ one's own inventory of sounds, in nonsense combinations, but with simulated "foreign" features. At least in West Africa and Latin America, the types of glossolalia employed seemed to fit into this description.[21]

The conclusions of the linguists indicate that modern glossolalia is composed of unknown sounds with no distinguishing vocabulary and grammatical features, simulated foreign features, and the total absence of language characteristics. The essential character of this new movement is therefore at variance with the Biblical phenomenon of speaking in known languages.

Summary

Various opinions are held as to the basic nature of the Biblical phenomenon of speaking in tongues. Some liberals have denied the miracle and redefined the phenomenon as the presentation of expository comments upon Old Testament texts. A few have held to the view that all tongue-speaking was in the form of ecstatic speech or unknown sounds. Many believe that the phenomenon consisted of speaking only known languages of the world. The position of the modern tongues movement is that tongue-speaking can be done in either known or unknown languages. Actually, the greater majority of modern tongue-speaking is in the form of unknown sounds.

The exact nature of the Biblical phenomenon can only be determined by the New Testament. The Greek term *glossa* is used variously for the organ of speech, a synonym for a race of people, foreign languages, and as part of the description of speaking in tongues. The term is used in nine different ways to describe the phenomenon. Lexicographers believe that the phenomenon could involve both known languages and ecstatic speech. However, the usage of *glossa* and the description of the phenomenon in the New

---

[21] Cited by Edman, *op. cit.*, p. 16.

Testament reveal that only speaking in known languages was involved. At least eighteen arguments based upon Scripture and logic were presented to support this conclusion.

Linguistic scholars have affirmed the fact that the modern tongues movement is characterized by the speaking of unknown sounds without any language basis. Therefore, the essential character of the new movement is not in accord with the Biblical standard. Consequently it cannot be of God.

CHAPTER V

TONGUES IN THE GOSPEL OF MARK

The only mention of the phenomenon of speaking in tongues in the four Gospels is found in the great commission as recorded by Mark (16:17). This becomes significant when one realizes that the Holy Spirit played a prominent part in the Gospel era.

The Absence of Tongues Elsewhere

The Holy Spirit was the agent of the conception of the incarnate Christ (Luke 1:35). At least five persons are said to have been filled with the Holy Spirit: Jesus Christ (Matt. 3:16; Luke 4:1), John the Baptist (Luke 1:15), Elizabeth (Luke 1:41), Zacharias (Luke 1:67), and Simeon (Luke 2:25). However, none of these are reported to have spoken in tongues either contemporaneous or subsequent to the experience of filling. John the Baptist predicted that Jesus would baptize in the Holy Spirit and in fire (Matt. 3:11), but he never mentioned that speaking in tongues would be the physical evidence of the experience. Jesus predicted that the disciples would be told by the Spirit what to say in the time of persecution (Matt. 10:20; Mark 13:11; Luke 12:12), but this is not the same as "speaking with other tongues as the Spirit gave utterance" (Acts 2:4). Jesus also predicted the advent of the Holy Spirit into the world and into believers' lives (John 7:37-39; 14:16; 16:7), but He nowhere intimated that it would be accompanied by the phenomenon of speaking in tongues. Jean Stone claimed that believers are expected to ask God for the Holy Spirit (cf. Luke 11:13) and that tongue-speaking will be the evidence of His reception.[1] Her claim fails to realize the transitional distinctives in the Gospel era. Christ later said that He would "pray the Father and He shall give you another comforter" (John 16:16). The disciples were not told after this declaration to ask for the Holy Spirit. Today, there are only two classes of people in the

---

[1] Jean Stone and Harold Bredesen, *The Charismatic Renewal in the Historic Churches* (Van Nuys, Calif.: Blessed Trinity Society, n.d.), p. 6.

world—Christians who have the Holy Spirit (Rom. 8:9) and unbelievers who have not the Spirit (Jude vs. 19). There is no third
group of Christians who have not the Spirit. The Gospels are full
of such transitional statements which were never intended to become
the normal pattern for the present age. At one time, Christ told
His disciples to limit their ministry to Israel (Matt. 10:5-6), but
after His resurrection, He commanded them to go into the world
and to preach to everyone (Matt. 28:18-20). Doctrine should never
be based upon these earlier, transitional statements. Christ also
outlined the future relationships of the Holy Spirit to the believer
and the world (John 14–16) without any reference to speaking in
tongues. At one of His post-resurrection appearances to His disciples, Christ "breathed on them, and saith unto them, Receive ye
the Holy Ghost" (John 20:22). This climactic event was not attended either by speaking in tongues. In emphasizing the events
of Pentecost (Acts 2), modern tongue-speakers have failed to give
proper significance to this initial reception of the Holy Spirit by
the disciples.

In the Gospel era, there is an approximation to speaking in
tongues in demon possession, with one basic difference. The demon
spoke directly rather than causing the possessed man to speak (cf.
Mark 5:1-20); whereas true speaking in tongues was performed by
the person's lips and tongue under the control of the Holy Spirit
(Acts 2:4). The similarity lies in the facts that a supernatural
utterance was being spoken and that the person was under the
influence of a supernatural being.

There may be a condemnation of the repetition of certain
unknown words or syllables (in which most modern speaking in
tongues takes form) in Christ's teaching on prayer in the Sermon
on the Mount: "But when ye pray, use not vain repetitions, as the
heathen do: for they think that they shall be heard for their much
speaking" (Matt. 6:7). Beare stated that the phrase "use not vain
repetitions" (*battalogesete*) involved a deprecation of any kind
of unintelligible utterance in prayer.[2] The verb consists of *batta*,
which is not a meaningful word but an onomatopoetic suggestion of
the sound made, and *logeo*, "to speak." Other related words are
"stammerer" (*batalos*) and "to stammer" (*battaridzo*). In this

---

[2]Frank W. Beare, "Speaking With Tongues," *Journal of Biblical Literature,*
LXXXIII September, 1964), 229.

context, however, Christ is not referring to a mere defect of speech, but to the repetition of meaningless sounds. Is this not what Paul condemned in the Corinthian church (I Cor. 14:9,11,19)? Since speaking in tongues is a form of prayer (I Cor. 14:2,14), would the Holy Spirit cause a believer to utter unknown syllables over and over (as many do) when the Lord Jesus condemned this practice? God does not contradict Himself. He always acts in accordance with His Word. This passage then takes on great significance when it is related to the modern phenomenon of speaking in tongues. It forms another argument for the view that all Biblical speaking in tongues was in the form of meaningful, known words and languages.

The Presence of Tongues in Mark

As stated before, the only clear mention of the phenomenon of speaking in tongues is found in Mark's account of the great commission (16:15-18):

> And he said unto them, Go ye into all the world, and preach the gospel to every creature.
> He that believeth and is baptized shall be saved; but he that believeth not shall be damned.
> And these signs shall follow them that believe; In my name shall they cast out devils; they shall speak with new tongues;
> They shall take up serpents; and if they drink any deadly thing, it shall not hurt them; they shall lay hands on the sick, and they shall recover.

Contention of the Tongues Advocates

According to the modern advocates of speaking in tongues, all five of these signs should characterize every believer. Brumback argued that "if 'He that believeth and is baptized' is true in any and every age of the Christian dispensation, 'these signs shall follow' must likewise be true in every generation and period of the church's history."[3] Brumback added that the phrase "them that believe" does not refer only to new converts, but to all Christian believers. He then defined the nature of faith and the condition character of the signs: "As long as the apostles and other disciples continued believing in the Lordship of Jesus over every realm,

---

[3] Brumback, *op. cit.*, p. 54.

'these signs' continued to follow them."[4] This then is the view of the modern tongues movement. If a Christian would only believe what Christ has said here and would submit himself completely to the Lordship of Christ, then he would see these signs in operation in his life. This could take place in any generation, including that of today. In fact, the modern tongues movement and the full gospel ministry are the fulfillment of Christ's prophecy.

There have been and are many godly men who have not spoken in tongues: Calvin, Knox, Wesley, Carey, Judson, Taylor, Moody, Spurgeon, Torrey, Sunday, and Graham. Brumback stated that this argument "is based upon men rather than upon the Scriptures."[5] This is true, and yet one wonders whether these great Christian leaders and others could be classified as men who have *not* acknowledged the Lordship of Christ in their lives. Certainly they have manifested more holiness and witnessed more effectively for Christ than many who have claimed to have spoken in tongues.

However, the real answer to this claim by the modern tongues movement is to be found in the textual authenticity and the doctrine of the passage itself.

Authenticity of the Passage

Many Christians are aware that the textual support for the conclusion of Mark (16:9-20) is weak. The two most ancient and best Greek manuscripts, the Sinaiticus and the Vaticanus, do not have it. Some fourth and fifth century Latin translations, the Sinaitic Syriac version, and some Armenian codicies do not contain it. Clement of Alexandria, Origen, and Eusebius all omitted it. In fact, Eusebius said that the most accurate copies known to him and almost all the copies available ended with the words "they were afraid" (16:8).[6] No Greek manuscript earlier than the fifth century has it. This external manuscript evidence definitely favors the omission of the passage, although it is not enough in itself. This omission does create a problem, as Cole wrote: "To end the Gospel with verse 8 is not only abrupt linguistically, but abrupt theologically."[7] This abruptness must be acknowledged, and yet accepted. Everett

[4] *Ibid.*
[5] *Ibid.*, p. 275.
[6] Cited by Everett F. Harrison, *Introduction to the New Testament* (Grand Rapids: Wm. B. Eerdmans Publishing Company, 1964), pp. 87-88.
[7] R. A. Cole, *The Gospel According to St. Mark* (Grand Rapids: Wm. B. Eerdmans Publishing Co., 1961), p. 258.

Harrison, professor of New Testament Greek at the Fuller Theological Seminary, concluded: "Transcriptional probability favors the abrupt ending. If the long ending were original, it is difficult to account for the loss of these verses in our leading MSS. On the other hand, given the abrupt ending as the original, it is easy to see that there was a felt need for supplementation."[8] And there was supplementation. There are at least four possible endings which are found in various Greek manuscripts. The best manuscripts end with verse 8. Others contain a short conclusion of about thirty words. The majority of late manuscripts include verses 9 to 20. There are still others which have verses 9 to 20 with an interpolation between verses 14 and 15. What is the conclusion to this external, manuscript evidence? One must agree with A. T. Robertson, the great Greek scholar and grammarian of the past generation: "So the facts are very complicated, but argue strongly against the genuineness of verses 9 to 20 of Mark 16."[9] On the basis of this poor manuscript support, doctrine should not be built upon this passage.

Internal evidence also supports the conclusion of the external evidence. Harrison cited some of the incongruities of the passage:

> The word for "week" in verse 9 is not the same as in verse 2. Mary Magdalene's background, given in verse 9, is hardly natural here after her appearance in the story at verse 1 without any such description. The reader looks for something to be said in these closing verses that will fittingly fulfill what is stated about Peter in verse 7, but all he finds is a series of generalities. Finally, although the material in verse 18 might conceivably be congruent with the place that the miraculous element holds in the Gospel, it is perhaps more accurate to see a thaumaturgical motif here such as one finds in the apocryphal Gospels.[10]

Gould pointed out certain linguistic differences when he wrote: "There are 109 different words, and of these, 11 words and 2 phrases do not occur elsewhere in this Gospel."[11] These are: *ekeinos, poreuomai, tois met'autou genomenois, theaomai, apisteo, meta tauta, husteron, blapto, sunergountos, bebaioun,* and *epakolouthein.*

In the face of this strong external and internal evidence against

[8] Harrison, *loc. cit.*
[9] Archibald Thomas Robertson, *Word Pictures in the New Testament* (Nashville, Tenn.: Broadman Press, 1930), I, 402.
[10] Harrison, *op. cit.,* p. 88.
[11] Ezra P. Gould, *A Critical and Exegetical Commentary on the Gospel According to St. Mark* (New York: Charles Scribner's Sons, 1913), p. 303.

the Markan authorship of verses 9 to 20, it is hard to understand Brumback who agreed with the conclusion of the aged *Pulpit Commentary*: *"On the whole, the evidence as the genuineness and authenticity of this passage seems irresistible."*[12] No modern Greek scholar would say that the evidence for the inclusion of verses 9 to 20 is "irresistible." Why would Brumback make such a bold statement? First, he believed that the Authorized Version was "the most trustworthy of all versions and the closest to the original of anything we have today."[13] This is a commendable position but he held it at the expense of deprecating the Greek text and the findings of Greek scholars.[14] Finally, the author received the impression that Brumback had to hold tenaciously to the integrity of Mark's ending in order to justify his view that speaking in tongues is an integral part of the great commission and that the phenomenon was to be a permanent part of church and personal life. His doctrinal position definitely determined his acceptance of this passage. This is bias, not scholarship. The proper attitude toward this passage by both advocates and opponents of tongue-speaking should be that of Robertson: "The great doubt concerning the genuineness of these verses (fairly conclusive proof against them in my opinion) renders it unwise to take these verses as the foundation for doctrine or practice unless supported by other and genuine portions of the N. T."[15] Therefore, to build doctrine upon this passage is untenable. The passage may be a genuine part of Mark's Gospel, but until more evidence is forthcoming, it should not be used to support any position.

Doctrine of the Passage

In two ways, the doctrine of the passage will not support the Pentecostal position either. First, it can be demonstrated that the teaching of the passage is inconsistent with that of other Scriptural passages. This fact further confirms the poor textual support of the passage; therefore it should not be used by the tongues movement to prove their claim of the permanent existence of tongues in the church. Second, granted that the passage is genuine, it can be shown that the neo-pentecostal movement is not fulfilling all of the signs mentioned.

---

[12] Brumback, *op. cit.*, p. 66.
[13] *Ibid.*, p. 57.
[14] *Ibid.*, pp. 55-57.
[15] Robertson, *op. cit.*, p. 262.

The first doctrinal problem of the passage centers in the nature of faith expressed in the phrase: "And these signs shall follow them that believe . . ." (16:17). The advocates of tongues have stated that complete belief in the Lordship of Christ will cause a person to experience these signs. But is this so? Is "belief in the Lordship of Christ" what Jesus meant here? In the greater context of this passage, the word is used of those disciples who did not believe that Christ had been raised from the dead and that He had been seen by Mary Magdalene (16:11) and by the two on the road to Emmaus (16:13). Later, Christ Himself in a post-resurrection appearance rebuked them for their unbelief of His appearances (16:14). However, belief or unbelief in the physical resurrection of Christ is not what is involved in 16:17. The immediate context is the great commission of Christ to His disciples (16:15). He commanded them to go and to preach the gospel to every creature. He further said: "He that believeth and is baptized shall be saved; but he that believeth not shall be damned. And these signs shall follow them that believe . . ." (16:16-17). Belief in the gospel message will bring salvation, and the lack of faith will bring individual judgment. The signs, then, were to follow those who *believe for salvation*, not those who acknowledge the Lordship of Christ in their lives (just some Christians). That belief for salvation is the intended meaning is further seen by the usage of the aorist tense in both verses (*ho pisteusas* and *ho apistesas*, 16:17, cf. *tois pisteusasin*, 16:18). Individual acceptance and accountability (singular person) are emphasized in 16:17; whereas these signs were to follow all believers as a corporate group (plural person). That signs were to follow those who believed and were baptized is a categorical statement. Every single person who believed the gospel was to perform these five signs; but the plain fact of history and experience is that no Christian has done this. Even the advocates of tongues do not testify to the fact of having all five of these signs in operation in their lives. *All* of these signs were to follow *all* believers. Note the plural article and participle (16:17). Also, the antecedent of "they" (16:17-18) is "them that believe" (16:17) for salvation. It does not refer to the preachers or the apostles (they are referred to in the second person "ye"; 16:15).

The second doctrinal problem of the passage centers in the nature of the signs which were to follow the believers. The first

was: "In my name shall they cast out devils [demons]." Evil
spirits were cast out by Peter (Acts 5:15-16), by Philip in Samaria
(Acts 8:5-7), and by Paul in Philippi (Acts 16:16-18) and in
Ephesus (Acts 19:12). However, there is no indication in the
Acts or in the Epistles that all believers practiced this. These three
leaders (apostles and/or evangelists) were the only ones to cast out
demons. The second sign was: ". . . they shall speak with new
tongues." Speaking in tongues was manifested by the disciples
(Acts 2:1-4), by Cornelius and his household (Acts 10:44-48), by
the disciples of John the Baptist (Acts 19:1-7), by the church at
Corinth (I Cor. 12-14), and possibly by Paul (I Cor. 14:18) and
by the Samaritans (Acts 8:12-18). Outside of these instances, there
is no indication of a general practice of tongue-speaking by believers. Also, it was shown that the usage of *kainos* rather than *neos*
demonstrated that the speaking was to be done in known languages,
not unknown.[16] This has not been practiced by the modern tongues
movement. The third sign was: "They shall take up serpents."
There is no illustration in the rest of the New Testament of any
believer performing this deed. Although Paul has been cited as an
example (Acts 28:1-6), it must be remembered that he did not
pick up the snake, but rather that the snake bit him. Oral Roberts
has a unique explanation of this verse:

> Taking up serpents does not refer to handling snakes. This was an
> idiom of the East that referred to enemies. It means what Jesus re-
> ferred to in Luke 10:19, "Behold, I give unto you power to tread
> on serpents and scorpions, and over all the power of the ENEMY:
> and nothing shall by any means hurt you." This was power enabling
> them to overcome their enemies who would attempt to impede their
> spiritual progress, or would seek to prevent their being witnesses of
> the Lord Jesus Christ.[17]

This figurative or allegorical interpretation of this sign is incon-
gruent with the literalness of the other four. The context demands
a literal interpretation. The fourth sign was: ". . . and if they drink
any deadly thing, it shall not hurt them." There are no limitations
as to the type of liquid consumed (note "any," *ti*). Also, the phrase,
"it shall not hurt them" (emphatic double negative *ou me*), is a
categorical statement. Those who believed in Christ for salvation

---

[16] See Chapter IV.
[17] Oral Roberts, *The Baptism with the Holy Spirit and the Value of Speaking in Tongues Today* (Tulsa, Okla.: By the author, 1964), p. 16.

could drink any thing and not be hurt by it. Again, history, both Biblical and Ecclesiastical, is silent about this practice. In fact, Timothy may have been harmed by polluted water (I Tim. 5:23). The fifth sign was: ". . . they shall lay hands on the sick, and they shall recover." Many accounts of healing without the laying on of hands are recorded (Acts 3:1-11; 9:32-35; 19:11). However, there are cases where the laying on of hands resulted in physical healing (Acts 9:17-18; 28:8-9; cf. James 5:14-15). But again, this was not a universal practice. In fact, why did not the Philippian jailer heal Paul and Silas of their stripes rather than wash them (Acts 16:33)? This is also a categorical statement. Whenever hands are laid, healing will result; but this is not the case, as Pentecostalists and "faith-healers" will testify.

Thus, it has been shown that all five signs are to be manifested by those who believed in Christ for salvation. However, this was not true either in the lives of Biblical characters or those of the modern tongues movement. The word "signs" (*semeia*) is used extensively in the Bible with multiple references, but these five signs are never applied to all believers. The word was used of circumcision (Rom. 4:11), a requirement for Jews (I Cor. 1:22), tongues (I Cor. 14:22), and Paul's signature (II Thess. 3:17). Signs were performed by God (Acts 7:36), Christ (Acts 2 :22), the apostles (Acts 2:43; 4:16,22,30; 5:12; 14:3; 15:12; Rom. 15:17-19; II Cor. 12:12; Heb. 2:3,4), Stephen (Acts 6:8), and Philip (Acts 8:6,13). Signs will be performed in the future by God (Acts 2:19), the anti-Christ (II Thess. 2:9), the false prophet (Rev. 13:13,14; 19:20), and the spirits of devils (Rev. 16:14). There is strong indication that these divine signs were temporary and limited to the opening decades of church history. One wrote:

> How shall we escape, if we neglect so great salvation, which at the first began to be spoken by the Lord, and was confirmed unto us by them that heard him;
> God also bearing them witness, both with signs and wonders, and with divers miracles, and gifts of the Holy Ghost, according to his own will? (Heb. 2:3-4).

Although the word "them" (2:4) does not appear in the Greek text, the understanding of the translators was correct when they inserted it. It is noteworthy that God bore witness to those who had heard the Lord directly (the apostles) and not to the second genera-

tion believer (note "*was* confirmed," not "*is being* confirmed").
The writer of Hebrews nowhere testified to the existence of signs and
miracles as the proof of the superiority of Christianity to ritualistic
Judaism. Although the Jews required a sign, Paul gave them none
but preached Christ crucified (I Cor. 1:22-23).

Concerning these signs, honesty must agree with Cole's conclusion:

> Whether or no such evidential manifestations were intended to be
> continuous in the life of the church, or restricted to this period, or
> sporadic, must be considered in the light of the rest of the New Testa-
> ment; in view of the uncertain textual evidence for this longer con-
> clusion, no dogmatic assumptions should be made from it alone.[18]

These signs are not found in the other accounts of the great
commission (Matt. 28:18-20; Luke 24:46-49; John 20:21-23;
Acts 1:8). Since they are not all found in the experience of the
early church, this passage should not be set forth as the intended
pattern for this age. Also, it is not right for the modern tongues
movement to select one of these signs and to emphasize it as *the*
sign of Spirit-filled living apart from the other four. It is either
all five or none at all. That is what the passage teaches.

Summary

The absence of the existence or prediction of the phenomenon of
speaking in tongues in the Gospel period is significant. Several were
filled with the Spirit without speaking in tongues. The Baptism of the
Holy Spirit was predicted apart from any mention of this phenomenon. Jesus outlined the relationship of the Holy Spirit to the
disciples without mentioning it. In fact, Jesus deprecated prayer
to God that involved unknown and meaningless sounds. This would
negate the claim that speaking in unknown sounds is the duplication
of the Biblical occurrence.

Advocates of tongue-speaking claim that complete belief and
yieldedness to the Lordship of Christ would produce these signs
in the lives of believers. However, this is inconsistent with the
experiences of many godly, yielded men and with the correct
interpretation of the passage itself. These five signs (Mark 16:
17-18) were to be found in the lives of those who would believe

---

[18] Cole, *op. cit.*, p. 262.

in Christ for salvation. The fact that they have not been found is evident from the Biblical record, the course of church history, and the current tongues movement itself.

Also, since the ending of Mark (16:9-20) has poor external, manuscript evidence and shaky internal support for its genuineness, doctrine must not be based upon this passage. Since no other Biblical passage teaches the permanent existence of these signs in the life of the church, this basic thesis of the modern tongues movement must be rejected. For all practical purposes, the Biblical doctrine of speaking in tongues must necessarily be limited to the data in Acts and First Corinthians.

CHAPTER VI

TONGUES IN THE BOOK OF ACTS

The Book of Acts furnishes a historical record of the early life of the church. It relates the advance of the gospel message from Jerusalem to Rome, primarily through the ministries of Peter and Paul. It records the first apostolic sermon (2:14-40), the first apostolic miracle of healing (3:1-11), the first persecution (4:1-3), the first defense of the gospel (4:5-12), the first chastisement (5:1-11), the appointment of the first deacons (6:1-7), the first martyrdom (7:54-60), the first missionary journey (13:1–14:28), and the first church council (15:1-35). The book then has a progressive and transitional character in that the program of God leaves the old dispensation of law, passes into the early life of the new church dispensation, and advances into a later, more mature stage. Within this historical record, four unique receptions of the Holy Spirit are to be found, accompanied by the phenomenon of speaking in tongues in at least three instances. These four historical accounts will be presented and studied; later, their significance will be set forth.

Accounts of Tongues

The Book of Acts contains three clear accounts of speaking in tongues (2:1-13; 10:44-48; 19:1-7). Because of certain similarities, two other passages (4:31; 8:5-19) have been suggested, with the latter one being more plausible. Certain questions will form the directives in the study of these historical accounts. Where did the phenomenon take place? Who spoke in tongues? When did they speak or what was their spiritual condition at the time of speaking? What were they doing at the time they began to speak in tongues? What signs accompanied their reception of the Holy Spirit? Were hands laid upon them in order to receive this experience?

Acts 2:1-13

The first account of speaking in tongues took place on the day of Pentecost (2:1). The day of Pentecost was so called because it was celebrated on the fiftieth (English transliteration of the Greek *pentekostes*) day after the presentation of the first harvested sheaf of the barley harvest. It was the fiftieth day from the first Sunday after Passover (cf. Lev. 23:15ff.). It was also known as the feast of weeks (Ex. 34:22; Deut. 16:10) and as the day of the first-fruits (Ex. 23:16; cf. Num. 28:26) because it was the day when the first fruits of the wheat harvest (Ex. 34:22) were presented to God. In later Judaism, this day was reckoned to be the anniversary of the giving of the law at Sinai.[1] This particular day of Pentecost was significant because it was fifty days after Christ's crucifixion and resurrection and ten days after His ascension into heaven (Acts 1:2-3).

This great event occurred in the city of Jerusalem. The disciples were told by Christ to tarry in Jerusalem for the descent of the Holy Spirit (Luke 24:49). This they did (Luke 24:52; Acts 1:12). Those who witnessed the phenomenon of speaking in tongues and to whom Peter preached his sermon were dwelling in Jerusalem at this time (Acts 2:5,14).

The sound of the presence of the Holy Spirit filled "all the house" (*holon ton oikon*) where the disciples were. What was this house? Morgan, following Josephus, equated "house" with the temple or one of the rooms of the temple.[2] The temple was called an house in the Old Testament (Isa. 6:4) and is so described by Stephen later (Acts 7:47). After the ascension of Christ, Luke said that the disciples "were continually in the temple, praising and blessing God" (Luke 24:53). On this feast day, one would expect to find them there. A crowd of more than three thousand (Acts 2:41) would more likely be found in the temple area rather than in an upper room or in the street outside the private house. However, there are definite indications that the disciples were simply in a private house when the Holy Spirit descended. The immediate context does mention an upper room in a private house (Acts 1:

---

[1] F. F. Bruce, *Commentary on the Book of Acts* (Grand Rapids: Wm. B. Eerdmans Publishing Company), pp. 53-54.
[2] G. Campbell Morgan, *The Acts of the Apostles* (New York: Fleming H. Revell Company, 1924), p. 24.

13-26). They would more likely be sitting (Acts 2:2) in a private house than in the temple. Luke later distinguished between "house" and "temple" (Acts 2:46; 3:1). It is difficult to say with absolute certainty just where the disciples were; however, it is certain that they were together in one place in Jerusalem.

Who spoke in tongues? Luke simply says "they" or "them" (2:1-4). Who are the "they"? Alford said that "they" does not refer to the apostles only, nor to the 120, but to *all the believers in Christ*, then congregated at the time of the feast in Jerusalem."[3] Most commentators believe that the antecedent of this pronoun is the group of 120 disciples including the twelve apostles[4] or the 120 plus the twelve apostles.[5] Since this group is mentioned in the preceding verses (1:12-16), this view seems quite plausible. However, there are definite problems with these views. The best position is that only the twelve apostles spoke in tongues when the Holy Spirit came upon them in this unusual way. First, the closest antecedent of "they" (2:1) is the group of apostles (1:26). Second, it need not be thought that the apostles spent all of their time with the 120 nor that the selection of Matthias immediately preceded the descent of the Holy Spirit. Third, Christ only gave the promise of the Spirit to the apostles. He said: ". . . I send the promise of my Father upon *you*, but tarry *ye* in the city of Jerusalem, until *ye* be endued with power from on high" (Luke 24:49; cf. Acts 1:2-4). Speaking to the apostles only, He predicted: ". . . *ye* shall be baptized with the Holy Ghost not many days hence. . . . But *ye* shall receive power, after that the Holy Ghost is come upon *you*, and *ye* shall be witnesses . . ." (Acts 1:5,8). There is no indication that all of the believers were to receive the Holy Spirit in this unusual way. Fourth, the observers of the phenomenon "marvelled, saying one to another, Behold, are not all these which speak Galilaeans?" (Acts 2:7). Can it be proved that all 120 were Galileans? The apostles were called "Ye men of Galilee" by the angels (Acts 1:11). Peter's speaking had a definite Galilean accent (cf. Mark 14:70). Fifth, would a charge of drunkenness have been hurled at women (Acts 2:13; cf. 1:14)? Sixth, there is no mention of the 120 in Acts 2,

---

[3] Henry Alford, *The Greek Testament* (London: Longmans, Green, and Co., 1894), II, 13.

[4] *Ibid.*

[5] R. J. Knowling, "The Acts of the Apostles," *The Expositor's Greek Testament,* edited by W. Robertson Nicoll (Grand Rapids: Wm. B. Erdmans Publishing Co., 1951), p. 72.

but there are references to the apostles (2:14,37). Seventh, the mention of "daughters" in Joel's prophecy (Acts 2:17) does not mean that women received the experience of Pentecost. To be consistent, one would have to say that sons, daughters, young men, old men, servants, and handmaidens had to be present. Can it be demonstrated that all six of these classes were included in the 120? Thus, the apostles were probably those who spoke in tongues on that day.

The apostles were definitely saved men. They had professed faith in Christ and had experienced divine illumination (Matt. 16: 16-17; John 1:41,45,49; 6:68-69). They were pronounced spiritu- ally clean by Christ and were regarded as different than Judas Iscariot (John 13:10; 15:3). Christ regarded them as belonging to Him and to the Father (John 17:10). Before the Day of Pentecost, these apostles had already received the Holy Spirit (John 20:22) and had been commissioned to preach (Acts 1:8). Therefore, this experience on the day of Pentecost was one which took place sub- sequent to their conversion. The significance of this fact will be set forth later.

What were the apostles doing at the time they began to speak in tongues? Modern advocates of tongue-speaking, who see a permanent and universal pattern in their experience, would have to say that the apostles were seeking and praying for the experience. This view is based upon the phrase, "they were all with one accord in one place" (Acts 2:1; cf. 1:14). However, it does not say that they were praying; this is only inferential. Actually, they were sitting when the Holy Spirit descended (2:2). Kneeling or standing was the normal posture for prayer; "sitting implies that the assembly of disciples was listening to some discourse. . . ."[6] It is difficult to say whether the apostles were even expecting the Holy Spirit on this day. Jesus did say "not many days hence" (1:5), but He did not pinpoint the exact day nor imply that it would be Pentecost. They were simply waiting for the fulfillment of Christ's promise. Unger wrote:

> It must not be supposed, as is often done, that the Holy Spirit came at Pentecost because the one hundred and twenty disciples tarried and prayed for Him to come. Nothing they did or said could

---

[6] R. C. H. Lenski, *The Interpretation of the Acts of the Apostles* (Columbus, Ohio: The Wartburg Press, 1957), p. 57.

in one iota affect the matter of the coming of the Spirit. They were not told to pray, but merely to "sit," to "wait" (Luke 24:49), which only meant that they were not to attempt any work of "witnessing" (Acts 1:8) until the Holy Spirit came to enable them. Of course, they prayed (Acts 1:14), and had wonderful fellowship, but all this was unconnected with the coming of the Spirit, who came by divine "promise" (Luke 24:49), at a divinely scheduled time (Acts 2:1), at a divinely designated place (Joel 2:32), in accordance with Old Testament type (Lev. 23:15-22).[7]

These apostles did not pray for themselves to receive the experience. They did not pray for one another. They did not lay hands upon anyone. They simply waited for Jesus to do what He had promised to do. The descent of the Holy Spirit would come, not in response to prayer, but when Christ willed it.

The descent of the Holy Spirit was evidenced by three physical signs: sound of wind, cloven tongues like as of fire, and speaking with other tongues. Ramm said that the signs appealed respectively to the ear, eye, and mind and that they were intended to invalidate any charge of deception.[8] Unger argued: "If Sinai was wrapped in smoke and flame when the *Law* was given to *one* nation (Exod. 19), was it to be thought strange that phenomena of wind, fire, and tongues of various peoples should accompany the glorious gift of the *Holy Spirit Himself* to herald the sublime message of unfathomable grace to *all nations*, and every creature?"[9] The sound from heaven (not the wind) "filled all the house where they were sitting" (2:2) so that they were completely enveloped, immersed, or baptized in it. Since the sound indicated the presence of the Holy Spirit, they were truly baptized in the Holy Spirit (cf. 1:5). This sound was heard everywhere and caused the multitudes to gather (1:6). Some believe that the sound of speaking in tongues attracted the crowd,[10] but it is more likely that a sound *from heaven* as of a rushing mighty wind would be heard than human speaking *from a private house*. Luke's usage of the singular *phones* (2:6) is better related to the single sound from heaven than to the multiple sounds of the apostles (cf. Luke 23:23 where human voices are in the plural). Also, the employment of the aorist tense (*genomenes*; 2:6) fits the single sound better than the continual speaking of the apostles.

[7] Merrill F. Unger, *The Baptizing Work of the Holy Spirit* (Chicago: Scripture Press, 1953), p. 57.
[8] Bernard Ramm, *The Witness of the Spirit* (Grand Rapids: Wm. B. Eerdmans Publishing Company, 1960), p. 77.
[9] Unger, *op. cit.*, p. 62.
[10] Bruce, *op. cit.*, p. 59.

The "cloven tongues like as of fire" (2:3) were not the fulfillment of the "baptism of fire" (Matt. 3:11). That baptism is a baptism of judgment upon the unsaved, not a means of purification for the believer (Matt. 3:12; cf. II Peter 3:4-13; Rev. 20:11-15). Jesus did not tell His apostles that He would baptize them in fire (Acts 1:5). Rather, these cloven tongues were a preliminary to the actual speaking in tongues. Their one single speech was going to be divided so that each could speak in another language.

Schaff called the third sign, speaking in tongues, "the most difficult feature of the Pentecostal miracle."[11] Did all the apostles speak at the same time in different languages? Or, did all speak at the same time in the same language, going from one language to another? Or, did the apostles take turns speaking? Because of these difficulties, Kuyper stated that the disciples spoke one pure language which all believers one day will speak and that the observers thought they heard them speaking in their respective native languages.[12] Vincent said that "the Spirit interpreted the apostle's words to each in his own tongue."[13] This position makes the event a miracle of hearing as well as speaking. However, this position creates more problems than it solves. No miracle of hearing is indicated in the literal language of the text. The disciples began to speak with other tongues (or languages) long before the crowd had arrived. This speaking was in the form of known languages or dialects which were understandable without interpretation to the unsaved observers (2:4; cf. 2:6,8,11; also see ch. IV). The apostles spoke in languages which they had never learned, but they did so apparently with a Galilean accent (2:7; cf. Matt. 26:73; Mark 14:70). Bruce said that the Galilean dialect was noted for its confusing of the various gutteral sounds.[14] This fact contributed to the amazement of the multitude (2:7). The multitude was able to recognize their native languages and/or dialects and to understand what was being spoken by the apostles. How they did is not so important as the fact that they did. The catalogue of language groups (2:9-11) revealed a wide variety of languages and dialects. This multiple speaking by the apostles also amazed them. The content of this tongue-speaking was the "wonderful works of God" (2:11). What this

---

[11] Schaff, *op. cit.*, I, 234.
[12] Abraham Kuyper, *The Work of the Holy Spirit* (New York: Funk & Wagnalls Company, 1900), pp. 133-38.
[13] Vincent. *op. cit.*. III, 257.
[14] Bruce, *op. cit.*, p. 59.

involved is not clear. It was not a substitute for the preaching of the gospel because Peter later gave that message (2:14-40). Speaking in tongues did not issue in the conviction of their sin; this came later (2:37). Apparently, these people were bi-lingual because they were able to understand Peter's sermon without interpretation or the repetition of the phenomenon. Thus, speaking in tongues was an integral part of the events of Pentecost. Various views upon the significance of this unusual experience will be expounded later.

Acts 4:31

After the first persecution, the Christians held a prayer meeting. "And when they had prayed, the place was shaken where they were assembled together; and they were all filled with the Holy Ghost, and they spake the word of God with boldness" (*elaloun ton logon tou Theou meta parresias*; 4:31). Several writers believe that this latter phrase is an equivalent expression for speaking in tongues.[15] However, if this phrase does refer to speaking in tongues, it is the only place in the Bible that it does. Outside of the Book of Acts, the word "boldness" (*parresia*) with its cognates always refers to freedom, openness, and plainness of speech, confidence, and boldness. In Acts, the word is used several times (2:29; 4:13,29,31; 28:31) in this same way. The same can be said of the verb *parresiadzomai* (9:27,29; 13:46; 14:3; 18:26; 19:8; 26:26). In this same context, speaking the word with boldness is related to a public ministry of healing, signs, and wonders (4:29-30). Also, the modern tongues movement claims that a person can speak, pray, or sing in tongues at any time after his initial experience of speaking in tongues which occurred when he was baptized in the Holy Spirit. If this be so, then why did the Christians have to pray to God to give them this experience again (4:29)? The only correct interpretation of this passage is that the disciples prayed that God might give them boldness to carry on a public ministry in the face of threats and persecution by the Jewish leaders. The phenomenon of speaking in tongues is not found here.

Acts 8:5-25

The second unusual reception of the Holy Spirit took place during the Samaritan revival. After the martyrdom of Stephen, there

---

[15] Beare, *op. cit.*, p. 238, and Martin, *op. cit.*, p. 12.

was a great persecution against the church at Jerusalem, causing the believers to be "scattered abroad throughout the regions of Judea and Samaria" (Acts 8:1). Philip went to the city of Samaria and preached Christ to them (8:5). His oral ministry was attended by miracles and signs—casting out of demons and physical healings (8:6-7,13). His ministry attracted the attention of the Samaritans, caused great joy, and produced saving faith in them (8:6,8,12).

The Samaritans were a mixed race with a heathen core (II Kings 17:14; Ezra 4:2). When the Assyrians conquered Israel, the northern kingdom (722 B.C.), they removed outstanding Israelites from the land and repeopled the region with heathen Gentiles (II Kings 17:24). This integration produced intermarriage with the Samaritan race (half Jew and half Gentile) as the result. The Samaritans also had a different religion from that of the Jews in Judea (II Kings 17:27; cf. John 4:20-22). These two facts of racial mixture and rival religion caused a great separation and intense hatred between the Jews and the Samaritans (Ezra 4; cf. Luke 9:52,53; John 4:9). These were the people who "when they believed Philip preaching the things concerning the kingdom of God, and the name of Jesus Christ, they were baptized, both men and women" (8:12).

Luke then gave this account of their reception of the Holy Spirit:

> Now when the apostles which were at Jerusalem heard that Samaria had received the Word of God, they sent unto them Peter and John:
> Who, when they were come down, prayed for them, that they might receive the Holy Ghost:
> (For as yet he was fallen upon none of them: only they were baptized in the name of the Lord Jesus.)
> Then laid they their hands on them, and they received the Holy Ghost (8:14-17).

There are several observations that need to be made about this unique passage. First, there was a definite lapse of time between the conversion and baptism of the Samaritans and their reception of the Holy Spirit. Unger tried to argue that the Samaritans were not saved before Peter and John came down,[16] but this is contrary to the plain, literal sense of Luke's report (8:12,14; cf. 2:41). Also, if the Samaritans were not saved until Peter and John came, why did

---

[16] Unger, *op. cit.*, p. 66.

Philip baptize them? Again, why were not the Samaritans baptized after their salvation experience with Peter and John? Baptism after salvation is the Biblical standard (2:41; 8:36-38). Second, the Samaritans received the Holy Spirit through the prayer and the laying on of hands of Peter and John (8:15-17). As the representatives of the entire group of apostles, Peter and John prayed for the Samaritans that the latter might receive the Holy Spirit. There is no indication that the Samaritans prayed for this experience or that they were praying at the time of this experience. There is no indication that Philip prayed for them. Also, the apostles laid hands on them (8:17). There is no indication that Philip, the evangelist, laid hands on them. The significance of these facts "makes the baptism of the Samaritans *without* the reception of the Spirit appear as something *extraordinary*: the epoch-making advance of Christianity beyond the bound of Judea into Samaria was *not* to be accomplished *without the intervention of the direct ministry of the apostles.*"[17]

The absence of the signs which accompanied the descent of the Holy Spirit on the day of Pentecost is conspicuous. There is no mention of the sound as of a rushing might wind nor of the cloven tongues like as of fire (2:2-3). Although speaking in tongues is not explicitly mentioned in the passage, many commentators believe that the phenomenon occurred then.[18] This position is based upon the usage of "saw" (*idon*) in the phrase: "And when Simon saw that through laying on of the apostles' hands the Holy Ghost was given, he offered them money" (8:18). What did Simon "see" that caused him to offer the apostles money? The usual answer is that Simon saw them speaking in tongues. Brumback admitted that this is circumstantial evidence, but he believed that the presence of tongues in other accounts would support his conjecture. He stated: "The burden of proof would most certainly seem to lie upon those who assert that speaking with tongues was not present on this occasion."[19] Are there any proofs that tongues did not occur then? Yes, there are some. First, the phenomenon is not mentioned in the passage. This fact takes on importance when one realizes that tongues are

[17] Heinrich August Wilhelm Meyer, *Critical and Exegetical Handbook to The Acts of the Apostles* (New York: Funk & Wagnalls, 1889), p. 70.
[18] Bruce, *op. cit.*, p. 181. Also Merrill C. Tenney, *The Zondervan Pictorial Bible Dictionary* (Grand Rapids: Zondervan Publishing House, 1963), pp. 859-60.
[19] Brumback, *op. cit.*, p. 214.

mentioned later by Luke (Acts 10:44-48; 19:1-7). If Luke wanted to present a pattern of receiving the Holy Spirit accompanied by speaking in tongues, would he have omitted this second reference to the phenomenon? It would have been more logical and natural to omit reference to it later once the pattern had been established. Second, the usage of "saw" is not conclusive. Speaking in tongues would appeal to the sense of hearing rather than of seeing (cf. 10:46). The phenomena of Pentecost were both seen and heard by the observers (cf. 2:33). Their argument would be conclusive if the record stated that Simon "saw and heard." Third, Simon simply *saw* that the apostles had laid hands upon them. He wanted this power which was performed through the laying on of hands (8:19). Actually, the burden of proof rests upon those who read into the text the phenomenon when it is not specifically mentioned. On this basis, one could say that the sound of wind and the tongues of fire were also present. This is subjective eisegesis, not objective exegesis.

Acts 10:1–11:18

The third unusual reception of the Holy Spirit occurred in Caesarea, a town on the sea coast of Palestine on the great road from Tyre to Egypt (10:1,24; 11:11-12). Cornelius, a Roman centurion and a Gentile, was told by an angel in a vision to summon Peter from Joppa. Meanwhile, Peter himself received a vision from God in which he was being taught not to regard the Gentiles as unclean or inferior. After hearing the report of Cornelius' ambassadors, Peter returned with them to Caesarea. After Cornelius reiterated his vision, Peter preached the gospel to him and his household. Luke then gave this climax:

> While Peter yet spake these words, the Holy Ghost fell on all them which heard the word.
>
> And they of the circumcision which believed were astonished, as many as came with Peter, because that on the Gentiles also was poured out the gift of the Holy Ghost.
>
> For they heard them speak with tongues, and magnify God. Then answered Peter.
>
> Can any man forbid water, that these should not be baptized, which have received the Holy Ghost as well as we?
>
> And he commanded them to be baptized in the name of the Lord. Then prayed they him to tarry certain days (10:44-48).

Several conclusions can be made from this passage. First, Cornelius received the Holy Spirit at the very moment he believed in Christ for salvation. Cornelius was not saved prior to this experience. Although he was "a devout man, and one that feared God with all his house, which gave much alms to the people, and prayed to God alway" (10:2), the angel still told him to send for Peter "who shall tell thee words, whereby thou and all thy house *shall be saved*" (11:14). Luke wrote that "while Peter yet spake these words, the Holy Ghost fell on all them which heard the word" (10:45). What is the antecedent of "these words"? In verse 43, Peter had just come in his message to the essential core of the gospel: "To him give all the prophets witness, that through his name whosoever believeth in him shall receive remission of sins." When Peter mentioned belief in Christ, the spiritually prepared hearts of Cornelius and his household responded in saving faith, and it was at that moment the Holy Spirit fell upon them. This experience is contrary to the basic thesis of the modern tongues movement. Thomas Zimmerman, general superintendent of the Assemblies of God, stated: "There are a number of Scripture passages [John 14:17; Acts 2, 8, 19; Eph. 1:3] which would indicate that believers do not receive the *infilling* or *baptism* in the Holy Spirit at the time of conversion."[20] However, Zimmerman never referred to this experience of Cornelius which in itself disproves his thesis.

Second, at the moment Cornelius received the Spirit, he was listening and Peter was preaching (10:33,44; 11:15). Peter did not pray for them that they might receive the Spirit nor did he lay hands upon them. There is no indication that Cornelius himself prayed to gain this experience. In fact, he probably didn't know about the phenomenon of speaking in tongues (note his previous silence and that of Peter on this subject).

Third, the evidence of their reception of the Spirit was their speaking in tongues (10:45-46), but again, the sound of wind and the tongues of fire were absent. In emphasizing the once-for-all descent of the Holy Spirit into the world at Pentecost manifested by these signs and the lack of two of them here, Kuyper wrote: "This confirms our theory; for it was not a *coming* to the house of Cornelius, but a conducting of the Holy Spirit into another part of

---

[20] Zimmerman, "The Pentecostal Position," *op. cit.*, pp. 3-7.

the body of Christ."[21] This tongue-speaking was in known languages, recognized and understood by the observers. How could the Jewish Christians know that Cornelius and his house were magnifying God unless they understood the language (10:46)? Also, the same words are used here to describe the phenomenon as at Pentecost (10:46; 2:4; cf. ch. IV). The content of tongues was also the same as that of Pentecost—magnifying God (*megalunonton ton Theon*; 10:46) or declaring the wonderful works of God (*ta megaleia tou Theou*; 2:11). This phenomenon astonished the Jewish Christians because they had not yet learned that God wanted the Gentiles to be saved too (10:45-46; 11:1-3,18). Peter told the Jerusalem church that the Holy Spirit fell upon them "as on us at the beginning" (11:15). This no doubt is a reference to the Pentecostal experience, but why did Peter have to compare these two events? Pentecost occurred about seven years before. Could it be that the phenomenon of speaking in tongues had not occurred since then? He certainly could have referred to the events of Acts 3-9 if those events indeed included tongues. This may form another argument for the absence of tongues at Samaria.

A fourth observation is that Cornelius was baptized in water after he had received the Spirit and spoken in tongues. This is different from both the experiences of the apostles (Acts 2) and of the Samaritans (Acts 8).

Thus, speaking in tongues played a major part in this introduction of the gospel message to the Gentiles.

Acts 19:1-7

The fourth and final unusual reception of the Holy Spirit took place in Ephesus under Paul's ministry (19:1). It involved twelve disciples of John the Baptist (19:1,3,7) who did not know that Christ had come into the world, died, been resurrected, and ascended into heaven (19:4) and that the Holy Spirit had come into the world (19:2).[22] They may have been converted under the Baptist's ministry in Palestine. After returning to Ephesus, they may not

---

[21] Kuyper, *op. cit.*, p. 132.

[22] Their answer to Paul's question implies an ignorance of the existence of the Holy Spirit. However, this is not the case. This usage of *estin* involves the sense of "given" or "come" to complete the meaning (cf. same construction in John 7:39). John the Baptist clearly taught the existence of the Holy Spirit and His future ministry (Matt. 3:11). As his disciples, these twelve would have known this.

have heard that Christ had come. They were still waiting for the Messiah. Or, they could have received their spiritual knowledge from Apollos (Acts 18:24–19:1) or from the same source that Apollos had. In either case, these disciples must be regarded as believers of the Old Testament type. Their designation by Luke as "certain disciples" (19:1) is one used by him to denote true believers (cf. 6:1; 9:10; 11:26). Also, Paul's question inferred faith on their part, but with a lack of spiritual graces and power (19:2).[23] Paul explained their awkward situation of being Old Testament saints in the New Testament dispensation:

> Then said Paul, John verily baptized with the baptism of repentance, saying unto the people, that they should believe on him which should come after him, that is, on Christ Jesus.
> When they heard this, they were baptized in the name of the Lord Jesus.
> And when Paul had laid his hands upon them, the Holy Ghost came on them; and they spake with tongues, and prophesied (19:4-6).

These twelve disciples knew that they were supposed to believe in one who would come after John. When Paul explained that that one was Christ, they believed in Him and manifested their belief in Christian baptism. They became New Testament believers and members of the true church. Had they died after Calvary and before this explanation, they would have been classified as Old Testament saints. Christian baptism was necessary because the baptism of John was orientated to Israel and the Jewish hope of the Messianic kingdom (Matt. 3:2; 10:5-7; John 1:31).

After Paul laid his hands upon them, they received the Holy Spirit and spoke with tongues. There is no indication that Paul prayed for them or that they prayed for themselves in order to gain this experience. This speaking in tongues was again in known languages (cf. ch. IV). If prophecy formed part or all the content of the speaking, then Paul must have understood it. Since Luke used the usual terms to describe the phenomenon (cf. Acts 2:4; 10:46), this is a logical conclusion. Again, there is no mention of the sound of wind or tongues of fire.

[23] This question, though important, is not essential to the problem of tongues. The aorist participle is literally translated "having believed." In syntax, it can be used of antecedent action ("since ye believed") or simultaneous action ("when ye believed"). If simultaneous, Paul was referring to the normal reception of the Spirit today (cf. Rom. 8:9). If antecedent, he was referring to the unusual, transitional way of receiving the Spirit (cf. Acts 8).

Conclusion

Four unusual receptions of the Holy Spirit are to be found in the Book of Acts. They took place in four different areas (Jerusalem, Samaria, Caesarea, and Ephesus) and involved four different classes of people (Jews, Samaritans, Gentiles, and the disciples of John the Baptist). The following chart will reveal that no two accounts were completely identical:

	ch. 2	ch. 8	ch. 10	ch. 19
1. Sound of wind	x			
2. Tongues of fire	x			
3. Speaking in tongues	x		x	x
4. Laying on of hands		x		x
5. Spirit received after salvation	x	x		x
6. Spirit received at moment of salvation			x	

Also, the disciples were either praying or listening to a discourse when the Spirit came upon them (2). Peter and John prayed for the Samaritans (8). Cornelius was listening and Peter was preaching (10). Paul had just finished his explanation (19). Because there are so many differences in the account, what conclusions can be drawn from this phase of the study?

First, no pattern or model for receiving the Holy Spirit today can be developed from these passages. If a pattern is sought, which chapter will give it? If Acts 2, then the laying on of hands is unnecessary. Also, the sound of wind and the tongues of fire should be present. Christians should likewise tarry at Jerusalem. If Acts 8, then the apostles must be called for their prayer and their laying on of hands (Philip and the Samaritans could not do it themselves). This is impossible today because the apostles are no longer here. If Acts 10, then the Spirit is received at the moment of salvation before water baptism and without prayer and the laying on of hands. If Acts 19, no prayer is necessary. What does all of this mean? As Laurin wrote: "We must not make the tragic spiritual mistake of 'teaching the experience of the apostles but rather experience the teaching of the apostles.' "[24] The experience of the

[24] Roy L. Laurin, *Acts: Life in Action* (Findlay, Ohio: Dunham Publishing Company, 1962), p. 157.

apostles is found in transitional Acts, whereas the teaching of the apostles is clearly set forth in the epistles. Today, a Christian is marked as one who has the Spirit (Rom. 8:9), whereas the unsaved man is the one who has not the Spirit (Jude 19). There is no lapse of time between conversion and the reception of the Holy Spirit.

Second, the transitional character of the Book of Acts must be recognized. Certain things happened in the early church which were only temporary in nature. They were never intended to become permanent patterns. Christians today do not worship God in a Jewish temple (2:46; 3:1). Christians need not sell everything they own in order to support the poor (4:32-37). Christians today are not struck dead instantaneously for lying (5:1-11). Prison doors are not opened supernaturally (5:19). Christians are not converted today through a direct revelation and appearance of Christ (9:1-19). These examples should be sufficient to show the transitional nature of this book. Since God was introducing a new dispensation, He did things in the early life of the church which were not necessary for the later stages of the Apostolic era or permanent church life. These unusual receptions of the Holy Spirit attended by various phenomena, including speaking in tongues, fall into this category.

Significance of Tongues

The significance of the phenomenon of speaking in tongues must be gleaned from the Biblical accounts. Once this has been determined, then the contemporary views as to significance can be examined. No theological system should be permitted to impose itself upon the Biblical record.

Biblical Significance

The Holy Spirit could not be given until Jesus Christ was glorified (John 7:37-39). Jesus prayed that the Father would give the eternal presence of the Holy Spirit to His disciples (John 14:16). Jesus said that the Holy Spirit could not come until after His ascension (John 16:7). When the Holy Spirit descended from heaven on the day of Pentecost (Acts 2), it was in answer to the prayer and promise of Christ (Luke 24:49; Acts 2:33). The various phenomena, including tongues, announced objectively the certainty of His advent, both to the apostles and to the unsaved

Jews. It was a sign to the Jews that Jesus was truly the Messiah, that He had died and was resurrected bodily, and that He had sent the Holy Spirit from His ascended position in heaven as He had promised (Acts 2:22-36). Since the Holy Spirit has come into the world to undertake His ministry until the return of Christ (II Thess. 2:6-7), the experience of Pentecost can never be repeated. Christ sent the Spirit into the world *once*. This coming can no more be repeated than the coming of Christ into the world at His incarnation. Thus, speaking in tongues was not the evidential sign of an experience which the apostles sought, but rather a sign of the never-to-be-repeated advent of the Holy Spirit into the world. This beginning of a new dispensation can be compared to that of the Law. When the law was first given by God, the event was accompanied by thunder, lightning, fire, smoke, and an earthquake (Ex. 19:16-18). However, when God gave Moses the second tables of the Law after the first had been broken, the phenomena were not repeated (cf. Ex. 34). This first experience of Israel with God and the law did not become a normal pattern. Neither should the first experience of the church with the Holy Spirit be expected to become a normal pattern.

If speaking in tongues did occur at Samaria (Acts 8), the phenomenon was a sign to the half-breed Jews of their necessary dependence upon and their subjection to the authority of the Jewish apostles. Had they received the Holy Spirit instantaneously at salvation or through the instrumentality of a Grecian Jew (Philip), they may have established a rival branch of Christianity in opposition to that of Jerusalem. Their racial and religious background makes this a definite possibility. Speaking in tongues, then, was the objective evidence that they had indeed received the Holy Spirit through the Jewish apostles.

At first, the gospel was not preached to Gentiles although Jesus had commanded it (Acts 2-9; 11:19; cf. Matt. 28:18-20). The Jews, including Jewish Christians, regarded the Gentiles as unworthy of salvation, common or unclean (Acts 10:9-16,28,34-35; 22:21-22). God had to teach Peter about the worth and "saveabilty" of the Gentiles before he would go to the house of Cornelius (Acts 10:9-35). After Cornelius and his household were saved, the Jewish Christians at Jerusalem remonstrated with Peter for visiting and eating with them (Acts 11:1-3). Thus, to show the Jewish Christians that Gentiles could be saved and that they were equal to the Jews before God, the Holy Spirit was given at the moment of salvation apart from apostolic prayer or of the laying on of hands. Speaking in tongues was the objective sign to the Jews that the Gentiles had indeed been saved and had received the Holy Spirit. This phenomenon convinced both the Jewish observers (10:45-46) and the Jewish critics of these facts (11:18).

The occurrence and significance of the phenomenon at Ephesus (Acts 19:1-7) were unique. Wuest said that "Acts 19:6 has to do with a special case where Jews had come into salvation under the Old Testament dispensation of law and now were receiving the added benefits of the Age of Grace, *a case which cannot occur today*"[25] (italics mine). Since these disciples of John the Baptist showed ignorance of the advent of the Holy Spirit into the world, an objective sign was necessary to convince them that Paul's explanation and their new step of faith were correct. Just as tongues announced the advent of the Spirit at Pentecost, this speaking in tongues convinced them that the Holy Spirit had been given.

These four unusual receptions of the Holy Spirit, evidenced by speaking in tongues in at least three cases, occurred when the gospel and the Holy Spirit were being introduced to four different classes of people who were in existence after Christ's ascension— Jews, both Christian and unsaved; Samaritans; Gentiles; and the disciples of John the Baptist. When the gospel was given later to members of these four groups, there is no record that the Holy Spirit was received in an unusual way attended by speaking in tongues. Thus these experiences were introductory and temporary in character, not permanent.

Evidence of the Baptism of the Holy Spirit

The position of the modern tongues movement is that speaking in tongues is the evidence of the baptism of (with, in, or by) the Holy Spirit. They equate the baptism of the Holy Spirit with the filling of the Holy Spirit and accept Torrey's definition of it: "The Baptism with the Holy Spirit is the Spirit of God coming upon the believer, taking possession of his faculties, imparting to him

[25] Kenneth S. Wuest, *Untranslatable Riches from the Greek New Testament* (Grand Rapids: Wm. B. Eerdmans Publishing Company, 1943), p. 109.

gifts not naturally his own, but which qualify him for the service to which God has called him."[26] This experience, different from regeneration, usually occurs after salvation. It does not involve an eradication of the sin nature, but it gives power and enablement for Christian service. Such phrases as "filled" (Acts 2:4), "receive" (Acts 1:8), "come upon" (Acts 19:6), "promise" (Acts 1:4), "endued with power" (Luke 24:49), and "gift" (Acts 2:38) all refer to this same experience. Pentecostalists believe that the Holy Spirit indwells a believer at the moment of salvation, but that He fills or baptizes them later. This latter experience is evidenced by tongues.

Although Torrey did not say that speaking in tongues was the sign of this experience, Pentecostalists have affirmed that it is. Brumback said that it is a "charismatic experience, i.e., it is of a transcendent and miraculous character, producing extraordinary effects which are visible to the onlooker, its initial oncoming being signalized by an utterance in other tongues."[27] The Assemblies of God do not regard speaking in tongues as *a* sign of Spirit baptism, but as *the* sign. That denomination passed this resolution: "Resolved, That this Council considers it a serious disagreement with Fundamentals for any minister among us to teach contrary to our distinctive testimony that the baptism in the Holy Ghost is regularly accomplished by the initial, physical sign of speaking in other tongues."[28] Although this is the majority opinion of the modern tongues movement, some Full Gospel people do not accept tongues as the only or necessary sign.[29]

The permanent, Bible pattern for all baptisms with the Holy Spirit is based upon Acts 2:4: "And they were all filled with the Holy Ghost, and began to speak with other tongues, as the Spirit gave them utterance." If someone should ask about the sound of wind and the cloven tongues of fire, this would be their reply: "And yet, despite the fact that there were many aspects of Pentecost which were peculiar to that day alone, never to be repeated, there were some things about the day that were established as a pattern

---

[26] R. A. Torrey, *The Baptism with the Holy Spirit* (New York: Fleming H. Revell Company, 1897), p. 24.

[27] Brumback, *op. cit.*, p. 184.

[28] Cited by Carl Brumback, *Suddenly From Heaven* (Springfield, Mo.: Gospel Publishing House, 1961), 223.

[29] J. E. Stiles, Jr., Letter to the Editor, *Christianity Today*, VIII (November 8, 1963), 17.

for future believers."[30] However, this is very subjective. Who determines what phenomenon should be permanent or temporary? Also, since the laying on of hands is not mentioned here, why has it become a part of their pattern? Dalton argued: "All logic demands that there be a distinct initial evidence that the experience of the Baptism with the Holy Spirit has come to the believer."[31] Is this not an argument based upon logic or reason rather than Scripture? There is no physical evidence for the experience of regeneration when the person receives the indwelling presence of the Holy Spirit. Assurance of salvation simply comes from believing God's Word (John 1:12; 3:16), the inner witness of the Holy Spirit (Rom. 8:16), and the resultant changed life (James 2:24; I John 3:14). Thus, assurance of a Spirit-filled life comes from a life of witness (Acts 1:8) and the fruit-bearing of Christian character (John 15:1-8; Gal. 5:22-23). Asking for physical evidence is walking by *sight*, rather than by *faith*.

How can one receive the baptism of the Holy Spirit? The statement of faith of the Assemblies of God reads: *"We believe* that the baptism of Holy Spirit, according to Acts 2:4, is given to believers who ask for it."[32] Hurst listed six spiritual requirements: thirst and seek (John 7:37-38; Matt. 5:6; John 4:14; Isa. 55:1; Jer. 29:13), have faith (Heb. 11:6), ask in prayer (Luke 11:13), receive (John 20:22), yield (Joel 2:28-29), and drink.[33] An examination of these commands and supporting passages will reveal that they have been taken out of context and misapplied. Jesus spoke of a thirst for salvation (John 5:14; 7:37-38) and for holiness in life and the world (Matt. 5:6). The command to "receive" was given to the disciples on resurrection evening (John 20:22). The key command of this position is "ask," but there is no record that the disciples, the Samaritans, Cornelius, and the disciples of John the Baptist asked for the experience. Many instructions of auto-suggestions are also given in order to make the experience come easier:

1. Help the candidate see that the gift is already given and all that he has to do is to receive it.

---

[30] Brumback, *What Meaneth This?*, *op. cit.*, pp. 196-97.
[31] Dalton, *op. cit.*, pp. 75-76.
[32] "Interesting Facts About the Assemblies of God," *The Pentecostal Evangel* (September 16, 1962), p. 12.
[33] D. V. Hurst, "How to Receive the Baptism with the Holy Ghost," *The Pentecostal Evangel* (April 26, 1964), pp. 7-9.

2. Lead him to realize that anyone who is saved through baptism is prepared to receive the baptism of the Spirit.
3. Tell him that when hands are laid on him he is to receive the Holy Spirit.
4. Tell the candidate that he is to expect the Spirit to move on his vocal chords, but that he must cooperate with the experience as well.
5. Tell him to throw away all fear that this experience might be false.
6. Tell him to open his mouth wide and breathe as deeply as possible at the same time telling himself that he is receiving the Spirit now.
7. Don't crowd around and give all sorts of instructions. Keep an atmosphere of unity and devotion and quiet.[34]

These preparatory instructions and helps are all foreign to the Biblical accounts. They are contrary to the spontaneity and the sovereignty of the Spirit's ministry. Such instructions could only lead to a human effort to reproduce a Biblical phenomenon. They would lead to a self-imposed and self-deluded experience (for example, "*telling himself* that he is receiving the Spirit now").

There are several other reasons why this position of the modern tongues movement is incorrect. First, they have confused the baptism of the Holy Spirit with the filling of the Holy Spirit. Unger gives six reasons why these two ministries of the Holy Spirit should be kept distinct from each other.[35] First, the baptism of the Spirit is a once-for-all operation, whereas filling is a continuous process. The command to be filled (*plerousthe*; Eph. 5:18) is in the present tense, indicating a repeated experience. The disciples were repeatedly filled (Acts 2:4; 4:8,31). But, the baptism is a single event (Eph. 4:5) and is referred to as completed (Rom. 6:3-4; I Cor. 12:13; Gal. 3:27; Col. 2:12). Second, the baptism of the Holy Spirit is non-experimental (not experienced), whereas filling is experimental. Baptism is something which God does for you without your knowing about it. Filling is an experience to be desired and to be achieved. Third, there is no command for anyone to be baptized with the Spirit, but there is a command to be filled (Eph. 5:18). Fourth, the baptism of the Holy Spirit is universal among Christians, but filling is not. Paul wrote: "For by one Spirit are we *all* baptized into one body, whether we be Jews or Gentiles, whether we be bond or free; and have been *all* made to drink into one Spirit" (I Cor. 12:13). The command to be filled with the Spirit (Eph. 5:18) implies that some were not filled.

---

[34] J. E. Stiles, *The Gift of the Holy Spirit*, p. 104. Cited by Kelsey, *op. cit.*, p. 80. Also see Appendix I for an illustration of instructions.
[35] Unger, *op. cit.*, pp. 15-20.

Fifth, the baptism of the Spirit is totally different from filling in its results. Baptism unites one to Christ and makes one a member of the body of Christ (Rom. 6:3-4; I Cor. 12:13). Filling produces joy, thanksgiving, submission, service, and Christian character (Eph. 5:19-21; Gal. 5:22-23). Sixth, the baptism of the Spirit is totally different from filling in the conditions upon which it is received. When a person *believes* in Christ *for salvation*, at that moment he is baptized in the Holy Spirit. When a believer is separated from known personal sin and totally yielded to the Spirit, he will be filled or controlled by the Spirit. Thus, when a person is baptized in the Holy Spirit, he is vitally united to Christ in His death, burial, and resurrection (Rom. 6:3-4; Gal. 3:27; Col. 2:12). This act of God gives the believer an exalted standing and forms the basis of his sanctification and victorious Christian living (Rom. 6:1-13). By being united to Jesus Christ, the believer also becomes a member of the body of Christ, the true church, of which Christ is the head (I Cor. 12:13; Eph. 1:22-23).

A second reason why their position is incorrect is because they have emphasized personal experience above Scriptural doctrine. Mahoney wrote: "It is not the doctrine of Pentecost, but the experience that has blessed millions. We do not need the theology of the Holy Ghost baptism. We need the power of that baptism. Then the doctrine will take care of itself."[36] This assertion is contrary to Scripture. It makes experience the basis of faith and practice instead of the Bible. Experience should not formulate its doctrine, but doctrine should give shape to the experience. In fact, many testimonies of the modern tongues movement about the baptism experience bear a close resemblance to the neo-orthodox position of crisis encounter. One wrote:

> You asked me why the Baptism of the Holy Spirit is prophetical rather than mystical. Mysticism implies man's search for God, through long meditations, etc., while prophecy refers to God "crashing through" not only to find man but to bless him, and to speak to him and through him.[37]

A third reason is that their experiences are contrary to the experiences of the Scriptural accounts. All instances of speaking in tongues in Acts were in foreign languages, known to the observers.

---

[36] Mahoney, *op. cit.*, p. 6.
[37] *Letter from an Anglican Priest to a Spiritual Child* (Van Nuys, Calif: Blessed Trinity Society), tract.

What is the situation today? Bach admitted: "Rarely does the experiencer speak in one of the world's known languages."[38] To be the same experience as that of the Biblical characters, the nature of the phenomenon must also be the same. Paul L. Morris, pastor of the Hillside Presbyterian Church, Jamaica, New York (a church once financed by bazaars, dances, suppers, bakes, vegetable booths), related that the Holy Spirit came in and took possession during a group prayer meeting. Later, when he went to bed, he then began to speak in an unknown tongue.[39] This personal experience is contrary to that of the apostles who began to speak in known languages at the very moment the Spirit came and took control.

Thus, the position that speaking in tongues is the evidence of the baptism of the Holy Spirit must be regarded as being unscriptural in origin and anti-scriptural in practice.

Fulfillment of Joel's Prophecy

Advocates of the modern tongues movement claim that their experiences and those of the apostles (Acts 2) are the fulfillment of the "latter rain" and the "former rain" predicted by Joel (Joel 2:23, 28-32; cf. Acts 2:16-21). They base their argument upon Peter's quotation of Joel and his statement: "But *this is that* which was spoken by the prophet Joel." (*alla touto estin to eiremenon dia tou prophetou Joel*; Acts 2:16). The former rain referred to the original outpouring of the Holy Spirit evidenced by the speaking in tongues and the latter rain is the outpouring of the Holy Spirit in the twentieth century in the charismatic revival, also evidenced by the speaking in tongues.

However, can the phrase "this is that" support this claim? Gaebelein argued negatively:

> There is a great difference between this word and an out-and-out declaration of the fulfillment of that passage. Peter's words call attention to the fact that something like that which took place on the day of Pentecost had been predicted by Joel, but his words do not claim that Joel's prophecy was there and then fulfilled. Nor does he hint at a continual fulfillment, or a coming fulfillment during this present age.[40]

[38] Marcus Bach, "Whether There Be 'Tongues'," *Christian Herald* (May, 1964), 10. Also see Appendix I.
[39] Harold Bredesen, "Discovery at Hillside," *Christian Life*, XX (January, 1959), 16-17.
[40] Arno C. Gaebelein, *The Annotated Bible* (New York: Our Hope, 1916), V, 108.

This conclusion can be verified by the very content of the quotation itself. Although speaking in tongues did occur at Pentecost, there is no indication that sons, daughters, servants, and handmaidens prophesied then (Acts 2:17-18). There is no evidence that young men saw visions or that old men dreamed dreams (2:17). There were no wonders in heaven or signs in the earth present (blood, fire, smoke, sun turned into darkness, moon turned into blood, 2:19-20). This prophecy actually refers to the future day of the Lord (2:20) and the last days of Israel's history (2:17; cf. Joel 2:23,32).

Symbol of the Universal Gospel

Philip Schaff, the great church historian, said that the Pentecostal speaking in tongues "was a symbolical anticipation and prophetic announcement of the universalness of the Christian religion, which was to be proclaimed in all the languages of the earth and to unite all nations in one kingdom of Christ."[41] A recent writer agreed that the message of "other tongues" or the meaning of Pentecost was to preach the gospel of Christ in all languages to all nations.[42] Although this *may* have been part of the purpose of God behind the phenomena of the "cloven tongues like as of fire" and the speaking in tongues, it cannot be demonstrated from Scripture that this is *the* meaning of Pentecost. Furthermore, this explanation of tongues cannot adequately explain the subsequent occurrences of tongues (Acts 10:44-48; 19:1-7).

Means of Evangelization

Some have looked upon speaking in tongues as a means of preaching the gospel to those whose languages they did not know. Laurin wrote: "The first generation of Christians needed by miracle what they could not acquire by development, namely, the ability to witness to Christ in multiple tongues, so they could multiply in numbers and advance from the beachhead which they now occupied to establish themselves fully in a hostile world."[43] Ryrie admitted that this was one of the reasons for the phenomenon of tongues in Acts."[44] Although asserting that speaking in tongues is essentially the initial, physical evidence of the baptism of the Holy Spirit,

---

[41] Schaff, *op. cit.*, I, 232-33.
[42] Harry R. Boer, "The Spirit: Tongues and Message," *Christianity Today*, VII (January 4, 1963), 7.

the modern tongues movement does believe that the content of tongues may have an evangelistic message to the unsaved.[45] However, it cannot be dogmatically stated that the "wonderful works of God" (Acts 2:11) contained an evangelistic message. The apostolic tongue-speaking did begin before the unsaved had gathered. When the unsaved did hear the tongue-speaking, it apparently did not present the gospel or bring conviction of sin (cf. Acts. 2:14-39; especially 2:37). The "invitation" was not given after the phenomenon of speaking in tongues was over, but only after Peter's sermon was preached. Also, when Cornelius and the disciples of John the Baptist spoke in tongues (Acts 10:44-48; 19:1-7), there were no unsaved present; therefore, the content of tongues could not have been evangelistic. The Biblical accounts testify to the fact that whenever the gospel was preached to the unsaved, it was entirely apart from speaking in tongues (cf. missionary journeys of Paul; Acts 13-20).

Sign to Israel

W. H. Griffith Thomas thought that speaking in tongues was a sign specifically and solely for Israel.[46] It was a demonstration of power to vindicate the messiahship of Jesus Christ. It was not intended for permanent exercise after the final rejection by Israel (Acts 28:17-31). Ryrie added that speaking in tongues was a sign of confirmation to the Jewish people of the truth of the Christian message.[47] It was a confirmation to both those who observed and those who received the gift. This position has some merit, but it must be worded carefully. Jews were present when men spoke in tongues (Acts 2:5; 10:45; 19:6). Tongues or languages were a sign to Israel in the past (I Cor. 14:21), and the gift of tongues partially had this significance at Corinth (I Cor. 14:21-22). However, Lightner overstated this purpose when he said that tongues was a "sign to faithless and unbelieving Israel and an authentication of the messenger and the message."[48] This may have been true at Pentecost (Acts 2) and Corinth (I Cor. 14:21-25), but it could not

---

[43] Laurin, *op. cit.*, p. 48.

[44] Ryrie, *op. cit.*, p. 113.

[45] Frodsham, *op. cit.*, pp. 38-39, 229-52. This can also be found in many contemporary testimonies.

[46] W. H. Griffith Thomas, *The Holy Spirit of God* (Chicago: The Bible Institute Colportage Ass'n, 1913), pp. 48-49.

[47] Ryrie, *op. cit.*, p. 113.

possibly be true at the house of Cornelius (Acts 10) and Ephesus (Acts 19). When tongues occurred in the latter two cases, only saved Jews were present.

In this connection, some have viewed tongues as a sign of judgment upon unbelievers because of their unbelief, with primary reference to Jews but also including Gentiles.[49] This is based upon the historical background of Paul's illustration and its application to the Corinthian situation (I Cor. 14:21-22). The idea is that even though tongues are spoken, observers will remain in their unbelief. Although it is true that some doubted and mocked the Pentecostal experience (Acts 2:12-13), yet three thousand who were attracted by the phenomena were saved through Peter's sermon (Acts 2:41; cf. 2:33). Also, when tongues were spoken later (Acts 10, 19), only the saved were present.

Speaking in tongues no doubt had some significance to the Jewish mind, but each account must be studied on its own for its particular degree of significance. Purposes vary with the accounts.

Authentication of the Message and the Messenger

Johnson wrote: "The gift of tongues is the gift of speaking in a known language for the purposes of confirming the authenticity of the message to the apostolic church."[50] Warfield believed that the spiritual gifts were the signs of apostleship (cf. II Cor. 12:12).[51] Apostles possessed both them and the ability to transmit them. These gifts gradually ceased as the apostles and the recipients of the apostles died. It is true that God authenticated the apostles with signs (Heb. 2:3-4; cf. Acts 2:43; 4:16,22,30; 5:12; 14:3,15, 12; Rom. 15:17-19). Tongues in a sense did authenticate the apostolic message at Pentecost (Acts 2:32-36). It would have vindicated apostolic authority at Samaria if it did indeed occur then (Acts 8:14-17). It would have confirmed Paul's explanation of the gospel to the disciples of John the Baptist (Acts 19:1-7). A problem of making this the exclusive purpose of tongues rests at the house of Cornelius (Acts 10) and the Corinthian church. Cornelius was prepared beforehand to accept the authority and the message of

[48] Robert P. Lightner, *Speaking in Tongues and Divine Healing* (Des Plaines, Ill.: Regular Baptist Press, 1965), p. 20.
[49] Lenski, *First Corinthians, op. cit.*, p. 600.
[50] S. Lewis John, Jr., "The Gift of Tongues and the Book of Acts," *Bibliotheca Sacra*, CXX (October-December, 1963), 309.
[51] Cited by Farrell, *op. cit.*, pp. 4-5.

Peter. The Corinthian church practiced tongue-speaking in the absence of any apostle and in the relative privacy of their own membership. Again, elements of truth are found in this position, but it can only be used of certain accounts.

Summary

In the Book of Acts, there are three clear cases of speaking in tongues (2:1-13; 10:44-48; 19:1-7). One other is possible (8:5-25), whereas a fifth alleged account must be rejected (4:31).

On the day of Pentecost in Jerusalem, the apostles spoke in tongues when the Holy Spirit descended from heaven (2:1-13). Their speaking in known languages was an objective evidence that the Holy Spirit had indeed come in fulfillment of Christ's promise and it was a sign to the Jews that Jesus was truly the Messiah and that the apostolic message was true. Other phenomena, such as the sound of wind and the cloven tongues like as of fire, confirmed this. The Spirit of God did not come as an answer to apostolic prayer or the laying on of hands, but at the sovereignly appointed time of the Father. Thus, the event was unique and can never be repeated.

In Samaria, the Samaritan believers received the Holy Spirit through apostolic prayer and the laying on of hands (8:5-25). This experience occurred subsequent to their salvation. If they did speak in tongues, it authenticated the authority of the Jewish apostles and revealed to the half-breed Jews their dependence and submission to them.

At Caesarea, Cornelius and his household (Gentiles) received the Holy Spirit and spoke in tongues at the very moment of belief for salvation. They were simply listening to Peter's sermon when the Spirit came upon them. There was no prayer, either personal or apostolic, and no laying on of hands. They were subsequently baptized in water. This phenomenon was a sign to the Jewish Christians, both present and absent, that Gentiles could be saved and that they were equal to the Jew before God.

In Ephesus, the disciples of John the Baptist (Old Testament saints) believed the further revelation of God in Christ as explained by Paul. After they were baptized in water and had hands laid upon them, they received the Holy Spirit and spoke in tongues. This phenomenon authenticated both the messenger (Paul) and the message to these disciples. It was an objective evidence that the Holy Spirit had indeed been given as Paul had said. Since there are no Old Testament saints living today, this experience cannot be repeated.

These four accounts served to introduce the Holy Spirit to four different classes of people. They were unique. They were never intended to become a permanent pattern for an experience to be sought by Christians. This is demonstrated by the facts that no two of these four accounts are completely identical and that the Book of Acts is basically transitional in character.

Contemporary views as to the significance of tongues were presented. Several of these were completely erroneous. Tongues is not the evidence of the baptism of the Holy Spirit, as the modern tongues movement claims. Both their concept of this doctrine and their personal experiences are alien to the Biblical record. Their misinterpretation and misapplication of Joel's prophecy must be rejected. The views that speaking in tongues was a means of evangelization or the symbol of the universal gospel must also be waived because of the lack of Scriptural support. That speaking in tongues was a sign to Israel and an authentication of the apostolic message and authority can be accepted, but only in certain passages where the Scriptures will permit these purposes.

The phenomenon, then, had multiple significance. Each occurrence must explain its own significance.

CHAPTER VII

TONGUES IN THE EPISTLE OF FIRST CORINTHIANS

The church at Corinth was established by Paul during his second missionary journey (Acts 18:1-18). During his eighteen months there, he encountered much opposition from the Jews, but nevertheless, the work increased, composed largely of Gentiles. After Paul left Corinth, many spiritual and moral problems developed within the church. Paul learned about these problems from the household of Chloe (I Cor. 1:11), a letter of inquiry sent to him (7:1), and the personal visits of some Corinthian believers (16:17). From Ephesus during his third journey, Paul wrote his first epistle to the Corinthians to correct the situation. What problems were in the church? There were divisions (1:11), carnality (3:3), wrong concepts of the gospel ministry (3:5–4:21), gross fornication (5:1), lawsuits between Christians (6:1), moral abuses of the believers' bodies (6:15), ignorance of marriage relationships (7:1) and the purpose of virginity (7:25), violations of Christian liberty (8:1), insubordination of women (11:2), abuses of the Lord's Supper (11:17), ignorance of the nature of spiritual gifts (12:1), and denials of the physical resurrection of the Christian's body (15:1). Stagg believed that the Corinthian church was characterized by the wisdom of the world (1:20), not by the wisdom of God.[1] This manifested itself in self-centeredness, self-love, self-trust, and self-assertion. An examination of the various problems discussed by Paul will reveal that the Corinthians were basically proud and insistent upon asserting their personal rights (doing what they pleased). It was this church that was rich in the possession of spiritual gifts (1:5-7), but ignorant of their nature and proper usage (12:1), especially that of the gift of tongues. Schweizer summarized well this situation:

> In Corinth a conception of the Spirit of God was predominant which mixed up Holy Spirit and enthusiasm. To the Corinthians, an

---

[1] Frank Stagg, "The Motif of First Corinthians," *Southwestern Journal of Theology*, III (October, 1960), 15.

utterance seemed to be the more godly the more miraculous it appeared. Thus glossolalia was the highest degree of spiritual maturity, just because it showed itself depending on a mysterious power which could not be identified with any natural faculty of man.[2]

This carnal concept was no doubt a remnant of their unsaved, idolatrous days when ecstatic utterances made by a pagan priest or priestess under the control of a false god were considered to be the pinnacle of a religious experience. In his first letter then, Paul gave much attention to the true nature of spiritual gifts with great emphasis upon the gift of tongues (I Cor. 12-14).

Tongues and Spiritual Gifts

In chapter 12, Paul dealt with the general nature of spiritual gifts. From this discussion, valuable information about the true nature of the gift of tongues can be gained.

Lists of Gifts

Although spiritual gifts are discussed elsewhere (Rom. 12:3-8; Eph. 4:7-11), First Corinthians is the only epistle that mentions the gift of tongues by name. A comparison of the various lists of gifts will show that "these gifts were not a fixed and unchanging catalog or just so many specific functions in the church."[3]

I Cor. 12:8-10	I Cor. 12:28-30	Rom. 12:3-8	Eph. 4:7-11
1. Wisdom	1. Apostles	1. Prophecy	1. Apostles
2. Knowledge	2. Prophets	2. Ministry	2. Prophets
3. Faith	3. Teachers	3. Teachers	3. Evangelists
4. Healing	4. Miracles	4. Exhortation	4. Pastor-teachers
5. Miracles	5. Healing	5. Giving	
6. Prophecy	6. Helps	6. Ruling	
7. Discerning of spirits	7. Governments	7. Mercy	
8. Tongues	8. Tongues		
9. Interpretation	9. Interpretation		

Sixteen separate gifts in all have been identified, with the admission that there may be others.[4] The first list (I Cor. 12:8-10) emphasizes the gift only; the second (I Cor. 12:28-30) both gifted men or offices and the gift; the third (Rom. 12:3-8) both the gift and the duty of the gift; and the fourth (Eph. 4:7-11) the gifted men or office. The order of the lists, although important, should not be

---

[2] Edward Schweizer, "The Service of Worship," *Interpretation*, XIII (October, 1959), 403.

[3] James L. Boyer, "The Office of the Prophet in New Testament Times," *Grace Journal*, I (Spring, 1960), 17.

[4] Rene Pache, *The Person and Work of the Holy Spirit* (Chicago: Moody Press, 1954), pp. 180-81. Also John F. Walvoord, *The Holy Spirit* (Wheaton, Ill.: Van Kampen Press, 1954), p. 168.

pushed too far. In the two lists where it appears, tongues and the interpretation of tongues are designated last. This would reveal the fact that they are regarded by Paul as the least of the gifts, but nevertheless, they are still gifts and important to the function of the body of Christ. In one list (I Cor. 12:8-10), prophecy appears after healing and miracles, but in another (I Cor. 12:28-30) it appears before them. Healing and miracles are also reversed in these two lists.

Definition of Gifts

Now that the spiritual gifts have been enumerated, what are they? Paul called them *ton pneumatikon* (12:1). This word grammatically can be either neuter ("the spiritual things") or masculine ("the spiritual men"). If neuter, it would refer to the gifts and their exercise (cf. I Cor. 14:1). If masculine, it would refer to the gifted men and their testing (cf. I Cor. 14:37). For all practical purposes, it is difficult to distinguish between the gift and the person who has the gift. Paul also called the gifts *charismaton* ("grace gifts"; 12:4; cf. Rom. 12:6). This term shows that the gifts have their source in the grace of God, whereas the former term *pneumatikos* reveals that the gifts are basically spiritual, not natural, in essence and that they are given through and controlled by the Spirit of God (cf. 12:4,7,11). A spiritual gift then is an ability given to the Christian out of the grace of God through the Holy Spirit and controlled by the Spirit in Christian service and growth.

What are the definitions of these nine gifts (I Cor. 12:8-10)?[5] Horton, a Pentecostalist, defined the "word of wisdom" thus: "The Word of Wisdom is therefore the supernatural revelation, by the Spirit, of Divine Purpose; the supernatural declaration of the Mind and Will of God; the supernatural unfolding of His Plans and Purposes concerning things, places, people: individuals, communities, nations."[6] The "word of knowledge" in contrast to the "word of wisdom" may refer to an imparted knowledge of God's will for the present whereas the latter may refer to the future. The gift of faith was the ability to believe what God has revealed and to act upon it. The gift of healings referred to the ability to heal the sick (blindness, leprosy, etc.). The gift of miracles was the ability to

---

[5] Excellent definitions and discussions of all the spiritual gifts can be found in Walvoord, *op. cit.*, pp. 168-88.

perform nature miracles as contrasted to physical healings. These healings and miracles authenticated the person with the prophetic gift. The prophet received a direct revelation from God (involving both wisdom and knowledge) and proclaimed it to the people with all of the authority of God behind him. The gift of discerning spirits was the ability to "discern the true from the false sources of supernatural revelation given in oral form."[7] All of these gifts are related to supernatural revelation, either in the mental reception of it, or the critical evaluation of it.

What was the gift of tongues (12:10,28,30)? One advocate of the modern tongues movement wrote: "The Gift of *Tongues* is an obviously supernatural means of God's communication with His people."[8] This definition then would coincide with the other gifts as being related to divine revelation. The tongue utterance is God's speaking to man, and the interpretation translates it for the common knowledge of the church. However, some tongues advocates disagree with their fellows in this definition. Oral Roberts said: "The gift of tongues has spoken to God in behalf of other believers, searching out inner weaknesses and needs, and linking them with the will of God and with the mind of the Spirit for them. The gift of interpretation gives God's *response* to the Spirit's intercession."[9] Tongues then is man speaking to God, not vice versa. However, the element of supernatural revelation is not entirely lacking. To one person is revealed by God the inner secrets of the congregation and these are voiced to God in tongues. The interpretation is not a translation of the utterance, but it is God's answer to the prayer; this is direct revelation (God revealing the truth directly to men). An important question about these definitions proposed by the modern tongues movement must be answered. Is God revealing Himself or divine truth directly to men today? Or, does God only reveal Himself and His truth through the written Word of God, as the believer is illuminated by the Holy Spirit? These questions will be answered in the next major section.

Another tongues advocate characterized the gift in this way:

> It is a supernatural utterance by the Holy Spirit in languages never learned by the speaker—not understood by the mind of the

[6] Horton, *The Gifts of the Spirit, op. cit.*, p. 63.
[7] Walvoord, *op. cit.*, p. 188.
[8] *What Next?* (Van Nuys, Calif.: Blessed Trinity Society), tract.
[9] Oral Roberts, *The Baptism with the Holy Spirit and the Value of Speaking in Tongues Today* (Tulsa, Okla.: By the author, 1964), p. 78.

hearer. It has nothing whatever to do with linguistic ability, nor with the mind or intellect of man. It is a manifestation of the mind of the Spirit of God employing human speech organs. When man is speaking with tongues, his mind, intellect, understanding are quiescent.[10]

However, Jesus said that a man should love God with all his heart, soul, strength, and mind (Luke 10:27). This involves all of man— his emotional, spiritual, physical, and mental faculties. Would Jesus then contradict Himself by causing a person to have a spiritual experience with a "quiescent" mind? Hardly, and Paul recognized this fact in his rebuke of the Corinthian manifestation (cf. I Cor. 14:14-16).

Others have defined the gift of tongues as an ability to preach the gospel in languages never learned.[11] Actually, lack of information precludes the formation of a dogmatic definition. Leon Morris wisely wrote: ". . . we cannot be certain exactly what form the gift took in New Testament days."[12] However, here is a tentative definition based upon available information. The gift of tongues was the Spirit-given ability to speak in known, foreign languages (not known to the speaker) in the public worship service of the local church. The content of speaking consisted of magnifying God which involved the revelation of God's character and His works. The interpretation involved translation and caused the people to be edified and to praise God.

The companion gift to tongues is the gift of interpretation (*hermeneia glosson*; 12:10). It has been variously defined. Roberts said that the interpreter gave God's response to the prayer uttered in an unknown tongue, although he admitted the possibility of simple translation: "Sometimes the interpreter explains what is said to God in tongues, so that the group may enter into the Spirit's intercession in their behalf."[13] Gee believed that the interpretation should generally resemble the tongues utterance and that it was "quite capable of being tested by anybody who might happen to have a naturally acquired knowledge of the 'tongue' spoken."[14] Horton said that the interpreter could declare the meaning or give a literal translation of the utterance.[15] The modern tongues move-

---

[10] Cited by Brumback, *What Meaneth This?*, *op. cit.*, p. 129.
[11] H. A. Ironside, *Addresses on the First Epistle to the Corinthians* (New York: Loizeaux Brothers, 1955), p. 385.
[12] Leon Morris, "Gifts of the Spirit's Free Bounty," *The Sunday School Times*, CVI (December 12, 1964), 6.

ment considers revelation, interpretation, and translation as all correct purposes of the gift of interpretation. Only the third possibility can be substantiated by a study of the word itself.[16] The gift of interpretation then is the God-given ability to translate into the language of the congregation the content of the tongues utterance. This is not done by the modern tongues movement because the vast majority of its tongue speaking is in unknown sounds which cannot be translated. Also, attempts at translating a known language have either failed or lacked objective confirmation.[17]

Source of Gifts

There is no doubt as to the source of the spiritual gifts; it is the triune God (Spirit, Lord, God; I Cor. 12:4-6). A gift is the "manifestation of the Spirit" (12:7). Specifically, Paul wrote:

> For to one *is given by the Spirit the word of wisdom*; to another the word of knowledge *by the same Spirit*; to another the gifts of healing *by the same Spirit* (12:8-9).

In summary, he said: "But all these worketh that one and the selfsame spirit, dividing to every man severally as he will" (12:11). These gifts then are sovereign ("as he will") impartations of spiritual ability to believers. They cannot be gained through human initiative, either in origination or development. They are not dependent upon human prayer or faithfulness. They are given as *He* wills to give, not as man wills to receive. Although the Holy Spirit is emphasized as the personal means or source of gifts, this does not necessarily exclude the Father and the Son (I Cor. 12:4-6; cf. 12:18; Eph. 4:11). It is God the Father who has "set the members every one of them in the body, *as it hath pleased him*" (I Cor. 12:18). It is He who has "tempered the body together" (I Cor. 12:24) and who has "dealt to every man the measure of faith" (Rom. 12:3). It is the ascended Christ who "gave gifts unto men" (Eph. 4:8) and who gave gifted leaders to the church (Eph. 4:11). The giving of the spiritual gifts is much like many of the works of God in

---

[13] Roberts, *op. cit.*, p. 92.
[14] Gee, *op. cit.*, p. 96.
[15] Horton, *The Gifts of the Spirit*, *op. cit.*, pp. 164-65.
[16] See Chapter IV.
[17] "Walvoord tells of a young seminarian who memorized one of the Psalms in Hebrew. At a tongues' meeting he stood to his feet and pretended to be speaking in tongues as he recited the Psalm. After he had finished, the interpreter woefully failed in translating what had been spoken." Cited by Ruble, *op. cit.*, p. 154.

which the Persons of the Godhead collaborated. If any distinction can be made, it may be that the Holy Spirit gives the abilities to believers and that God the Father through the Son gives the gifted men to the church.

Since God is the same yesterday, today and forever, the modern tongues movement claims that these gifts are possible today and are in fact being given. They say that the position that the gift of tongues ceased in the apostolic era is opposed to the sovereign will of God who can do today what He did then ("as he will" and "as it hath pleased him," 12:11,18). Lightner gave a candid and provoking reply to this assertion:

> Does this mean that the Holy Spirit of God is not able to do today what He did in the days of the early church? No, this does not limit the Spirit of God; actually it exalts His sovereignty, *for it means that He does not choose to do today what He did in the early church.*[18] (Italics mine.)

To say that God must do today what He did yesterday or in the apostolic era is to put a limitation upon God. This is contrary to the character of God and the events of Biblical and post-Biblical history. Although God does not change in His Person or nature (Mal. 3:10), His dealings with men do change. His witness to the world changed from being centered in Israel to that in the church. He will deal with sin in the future as He never has done in the past (cf. Rev. 6-20). God is immutable, but He is not immobile. It is not a question as to whether God *can* give the gift of tongues today; He still has that power. The question is whether it is God's purpose to continue the same phenomena that the apostolic church experienced. The claim that God must do today what He did then in response to the prayers of Christians is begging the question. The believer puts himself into the position of telling God what He ought to do.

Recipients of Gifts

Here is Paul's description of the recipients:

> But the manifestation of the Spirit is given to *every man* to profit withal.
>
> For to *one* is given by the Spirit the word of wisdom; to *another* the word of knowledge by the same Spirit;

[18] Lightner, *op. cit.*, p. 14.

To *another* faith by the same Spirit, to *another* the gifts of healing by the same Spirit;

To *another* the working of miracles; to *another* prophecy; to *another* discerning of spirits; to *another* divers kinds of tongues; to *another* the interpretation of tongues:

But all these worketh that one and the selfsame Spirit, dividing to *every man* severally as he will (I Cor. 12:7-11).

Emphasis is placed upon the individual, and upon every individual. This is also seen in Romans 12:3 (". . . according as God hath dealt to *every man* the measure of faith") and Ephesians 4:7 ("But unto *every one of us* is given grace according to the measure of the gift of Christ"). To whom does "every" refer? Horton said: "Not every man who is born. Not every man who is born again, for we must twice limit the circle; but every man who is filled with the Spirit as these Corinthians were."[19] Horton's statement is partially true. Unsaved men are not the recipients of these spiritual gifts; but every saved person is. It cannot be limited to a certain class of saved men—those who have been filled or baptized in the Holy Spirit evidenced by speaking in tongues. Paul simply does not say this. Paul regards "every man" as a member of the body of Christ (I Cor. 12:12,14,27; Rom. 12:4-5). At the very moment God "set the members every one of them in the body" (I Cor. 12:18), He gave to that person a gift that he might function in the body. At the moment of salvation through the baptism in the Holy Spirit, every believer is placed into the body of Christ. It does not depend upon his subsequent spirituality or filling. The Corinthian believers were members of the body (I Cor. 12:27), and they were carnal, proud, ignorant, and sinful. Every believer possesses each aspect of the unity of the Spirit: one body (Body of Christ or the true church), one Spirit (indwelling ministry), one hope of calling, one Lord, one faith, one baptism (baptism in the Holy Spirit), and one God and Father (Eph. 4:3-6). There is no believer who has just a few of these. If he has *believed* in the *Lord* Jesus, he has also been *baptized* in the *Spirit* into the *body* of Christ.

How many gifts does the believer possess? A tongues advocate wrote: "Do not be alarmed if you do not immediately see all of the gifts operating in your life. God will develop these abilities in you as you are ready and as need for them arises."[20] Did Paul

---

[19] Horton, *The Gifts of the Spirit, op. cit.*, p. 29.
[20] *What Next?, loc. cit.*

mean that *every* believer should have *every* gift? This cannot be gleaned from his usage of "every," "one," and "another" (*ekasto, ho, allo, hetero*; 12:7-11). His illustration of the body and members would argue against this position. Each member performs its own function and must not be expected to fulfill that of another. A hand can't do the work of a foot. In a series of questions which demand a negative answer,[21] Paul revealed that believers do not, and can not, have the same gifts (I Cor. 12:29-30):

> Are all apostles? are all prophets? are all teachers? are all workers of miracles?
> Have all the gifts of healing? do all speak with tongues? do all interpret?

It should not be expected that every believer should speak with tongues any more than that they should be apostles. The body of Christ is to be in perfect balance, and yet the modern tongues movement admits to an abundance of the minor gifts (tongues, interpretation, prophecy, and healings) and a lack of the greater gifts.[22] Since God tempers the body together (I Cor. 12:24) and gives it perfect symmetry, why does this group have a distorted ratio of gifts? If God were truly the source of these manifestations today, would there not be a balance and a greater presence of the best gifts?

Do all speak with tongues? No, they do not. Many have used this question to disprove the Pentecostal position that speaking in tongues is the evidence of the baptism in the Holy Spirit. Paul stated that *all* were baptized in one Spirit into one body (I Cor. 12:13) but that not all speak with tongues (I Cor. 12:30). The Pentecostalist will reply that everyone who has been baptized in the Holy Spirit *will* speak in tongues. He further states that in verse 30, Paul is referring to the gift of tongues which is exercised in the local church. Not all have this gift. The Pentecostalist makes a definite distinction between the evidential sign of tongue-speaking and the gift of tongues. However, their concept of the doctrine of the baptism in the Holy Spirit was proved false (see ch. VI). What is left is their concept of the gifts, and Paul said that not all speak with tongues. However, they state that this gift is possible for all

---

[21] H. E. Dana and Julius R. Mantey, *A Manual Grammar of the Greek New Testament* (New York: The Macmillan Company, 1953), p. 265.
[22] Dalton, *op. cit.*, pp. 82, 118. Also Albert L. Hoy, "Flame in the Sanctuary," *The Pentecostal Herald* (April 26, 1964), p. 14.

and therefore should be sought. This is contrary to Paul's clear declaration. "And if they were all one member, where were the body" (I Cor. 12:19)?

Purpose and Permanence of Gifts

The simplest explanation is that gifts were given in order that the members of the body of Christ, the true church, might function properly and harmoniously (I Cor. 12:12-27; Rom. 12:3-8). In addition, some gifted leaders had the responsibility of equipping other saints for the work of the ministry (Eph. 4:11-12). In fact, the church was "built upon the foundation of the apostles and prophets," certain gifted leaders (Eph. 2:20). More specifically, Laurin wrote: "The purpose of the gifts of the Holy Spirit was to fill the vacuum that would occur between the establishment of the church and the ultimate maturity of the church. . . ."[23] Since the New Testament was not written and since there were few apostles and prophets around, God revealed Himself and His truth through these gifts. Once the New Testament was completed and circulated, the need and the purpose of these gifts were removed.

Thus, some spiritual gifts must be regarded as temporary, limited to the apostolic era, whereas others were to be a permanent part of church life. Hodges has well stated this fact:

> Accordingly, inasmuch as Protestant theology generally has clearly recognized the cessation of the apostolic gift in the first century, at the same time that it rightly denies any form of apostolic succession, all such Protestant theology becomes basically committed to the *principle* of temporary gift. For clearly the apostleship was itself temporary, and, if the principle be established, it is perfectly legitimate to inquire whether there may not be other first-century gifts which were likewise temporary.[24]

The principle of temporary gift must be acknowledged. The gift of apostleship ceased when the last apostle died. This does not prove that the gift of tongues was temporary, but it does make it possible that the gift of tongues ceased when the last tongues-speakers died. This possibility must likewise be acknowledged. How can the gifts be classified as either permanent or temporary? After the gift has been defined, it must be decided whether its divine purpose is

[23] Laurin, *op. cit.*, p. 148. Also Boyer, *op. cit.*, p. 18. Boyer added the idea of confirmation of the preached word before the completion of the canon.
[24] Zane C. Hodges, "The Purpose of Tongues," *Bibliotheca Sacra*, CXX (July-September, 1963), 227.

still needed. If it is, then the gift must be permanent and it should be seen throughout church history because the true church would have not been able to function apart from it. If the purpose is no longer needed, then the gift was temporary and it will not be seen throughout church history. If the gift of tongues involved the revelation of truth from God to man or about man, then its purpose is no longer needed because God has completed His revelation (Rev. 22:18-19). The need for today is to understand what He has already revealed, not to have new revelation. The silence of church history will confirm the fact that the gift of tongues was not intended to become a permanent part of church life. Otherwise, how could the church of Jesus Christ have functioned in those centuries of silence?[25]

Relative Importance of Gifts

Paul told the Corinthians to covet the best gifts (*kreittona*; 12:31) or the greatest gifts (*meidzona* in the better manuscripts). What are the best gifts? Oral Roberts wrote: "Is it not the gift needed at the time? . . . If the need were for edification, would not the gift of tongues and interpretation be best?"[26] Necessity may be the standard of greatness, but one would question whether tongues is necessary today or is the best gift for edification (cf. I Cor. 14:3). The emphasis of Paul is upon the edification of fellow believers (I Cor. 12:7; 14:3,4,5,6,12,19,26,31). Those gifts which bring the most edification to fellow believers must be regarded as the best gifts. At Corinth, forth-telling (prophesying) and teaching were needed for the edification of the carnal, ignorant believers. Tongues, by itself, was regarded as a lesser gift than prophecy. It only had value when an interpretation accompanied it (I Cor. 14:5). However, it still took two to equal one. In this context of importance, Paul wrote: "And God hath set some in the church, first apostles, secondarily prophets, thirdly teachers, after that miracles, then gifts of healings, helps, governments, diversities of tongues" (I Cor. 12:28). Here, tongues is placed last and regarded as the least of the gifts, although it must be recognized as a gift and an essential part of the body of Christ at that time. The very fact that the Corinthians sought the gift of tongues reveals

---

[25] Further discussion of the temporary nature of tongues will be found under I Corinthians 13:8 ("Permanence of Love").
[26] Roberts, *op. cit.*, p. 55.

that their desires were prompted by their carnal natures, not by the Spirit of God. Likewise, the current emphasis upon the gift of tongues at the expense of the best gifts shows that the Holy Spirit did not create this desire. The Holy Spirit would not emphasize what Paul had deemphasized. Would He give to the modern tongues movement an abundance of the least gifts at the expense of the best gifts?

Tongues and Love

Chapter 13 should not be regarded as a parenthetical discourse on love. Rather, it forms part of Paul's treatment of the spiritual gifts and contributes much to the tongues question.

Necessity of Love to Gifts

Why did Paul introduce the subject of love? What is its connection to the problem of spiritual gifts? What is the "more excellent way" (12:31)? Lightner wrote:

> Paul is not attempting to show the Corinthians how to exercise the spiritual gifts, but he is showing them in this chapter the contrast between a life of gift-searching and a life of love-making. He is showing them a fork in the road—there is the way of gifts and there is the way of love. . . .[27]

Lightner believed that a choice had to be made by the Corinthians. They could either seek gifts or pursue love. The modern tongues movement is opposed to this view. Brumback stated: "There is no contrast between the gifts and love, save in the matter of permanence. . . the contrast is between the gifts with love and the operation of the gifts without love."[28] The inadequate way is to exercise spiritual gifts without love; the more excellent way is to exercise the gifts in the proper attitude of love for God and the fellow believer. Are these two views irreconcilable or can they be harmonized? Paul did give a twofold command to pursue love and to desire spiritual gifts (14:1). He stated: "Though I speak with the tongues of men and of angels, and have not love, I am become as sounding brass, or a tinkling cymbal" (13:1). If tongue speaking is not done with love, it is worthless, of no profit (12:7), and does not issue in edification (14:26). However, would

[27] Lightner, *op. cit.*, p. 55. Also Leon Morris, *The First Epistle of Paul to the Corinthians* (Grand Rapids: Wm. B. Eerdmans Publishing Co., 1958), p. 180.
[28] Brumback, *What Meaneth This?*, *op. cit.*, p. 158. Also Roberts, *op. cit.*, p. 69.

the Spirit of God cause a person to speak in tongues without also producing love in that person? No. God would not need to give a supernatural utterance through a person who had no love. If He did, He would be wasting effort and deceiving people because the utterance would not be profitable. Therefore, any speaking in tongues without love must be repudiated as being false. On this basis, John R. Rice insisted that the Corinthians did *not* have the gift of tongues at all.[29] On the other side, this cannot be a simple contrast between gifts with love and gifts without love. This would not explain how love *per se* could continue after the gifts cease. Even tongues advocates would insist that believers who have the indwelling Spirit develop the fruit of the Spirit (including love, Gal. 5:22-23) even before they receive the baptism in the Holy Spirit. This chapter gives a description of the type of love that should be present in the believer's life at all times, not just when he is exercising a spiritual gift. Therefore, the two positions can be somewhat harmonized.

Nature of Love in Gifts

The nature of divinely imparted love is set forth in verses four to six. It is a perfect expression of the entire fruit of the Spirit (Gal. 5:22-23). When a person is controlled by the indwelling Spirit, this love will be produced in the believer's life and will be manifested in all that the believer does. Each descriptive phrase can be applied to the exercise of the spiritual gifts. If a person does not manifest each characteristic, it is a sure sign that he is trying to reproduce the spiritual gift in his own energy. "Love suffers long." A tongue speaker will wait his turn to speak and will not burst into speaking at any time (cf. 14:27-28). "Love envieth not." Believers should covet or desire that the best spiritual gifts be exercised among them (12:31; 14:1), but a person should not covet a gift which God has not been pleased to give him (12:7,11,18). The foot should not aspire to be the tongue. "Love vaunteth not itself, is not puffed up." A tongues speaker should not be proud or think that he is someone special. "Love doth not behave itself unseemly." Speaking in tongues should be done decently and in order (14:40; cf. 14:23). Shaking and physical convulsions are unseemly. "Love seeketh not her own." The modern tongues move-

---

[29] John R. Rice, "Should One Talk in Tongues to Edify Self?" *The Sword of the Lord* (September 19, 1952).

ment believes that speaking in tongues can be done privately for self-edification. However, were the gifts given that only the possessors would reap benefit? Is this not selfish? Rather, were they not given for the edification and the profit of the entire body of Christ? Self-edification may be a by-product of the gift, but it should never be the goal (14:4,12).

Therefore, genuine speaking in tongues today should manifest all of these qualities. However, these qualities are not seen today. This is another evidence that speaking in tongues is simulated today, and not divinely motivated.

Permanence of Love and Temporal Gifts

In the last six verses of the chapter, Paul contrasted the permanence of love with the temporal nature of spiritual gifts:

> Love never faileth: but whether there be prophecies they shall fail; whether there be tongues, they shall cease: whether there be knowledge, it shall vanish away.
> For we know in part, and we prophesy in part.
> But when that which is perfect is come, then that which is in part shall be done away.

> And now abideth faith, hope, love, these three: but the greatest of these is love (13:8,13).

It is clearly stated that tongues *shall* cease, but *when* they shall cease is the problem. Several views have been put forth.

Since the immediate context deals with love, some believe that the spiritual gifts will cease when love is fully developed in the person's life. "Wholeness ["that which is perfect," *to teleion*] here is Agape [love] and what the Apostle is speaking of is something which is already taking place in time."[30] The word *teleion* does refer to the end of a process or development. In this book, Paul did use the word of mature believers (2:6) and he encouraged the carnal, immature Corinthians to become men (mature or perfect, *teleioi*, 12:20). His personal allusion to physical and mental development (13:11) would illustrate Christian development from infancy to maturity. The "childish things" would be the spiritual gifts which should be supplanted by mature understanding (13:11; cf. 14:20). Laurin said that verse 12 "may have reference to

---

[30]Nils Johansson, "I Cor. XIII and I Cor. XIV," *New Testament Studies*, X (April, 1964), 389.

heaven when it will be God's face and my face. We believe it comes *now*, when love will reflect a perfect image and reveal a perfect knowledge."[31] Although this position has some merit, it would be difficult to prove that no mature believer in the apostolic era had a spiritual gift.[32]

The position of the modern tongues movement is that the spiritual gifts, including tongues, will cease at the second coming of Jesus Christ; therefore, they should and are being experienced today.[33] They argue that the phrase "that which is perfect" refers to the perfect age which will be ushered in by the second coming. However, the word *teleion* is never used in the New Testament to depict the second coming, the millennium, or the eternal state. Also, since *teleion* is set in contrast to that which is "in part" (*ek merous*), it must refer to the culmination of a process. The second coming is not a process; it is an instantaneous event. A second argument is based upon First Corinthians 1:7: "So that ye come behind in no gift: waiting for the coming of our Lord Jesus Christ." They state that these gifts will last as long as believers are waiting for Christ. However, Paul did not say explicitly that the gifts would last until Christ's second advent. He simply stated the present condition of the Corinthian believers. They had all the gifts and they were waiting for the Lord. A third argument is that tongues were given to the church, and since they are the church, they can have tongues today. However, this is based upon faulty logic and is contrary to Scriptural teaching. Apostles were also given to the church, but there are no apostles today. The continuance of the sign of tongues as an intergral part of the great commission (Mark 16:15-20) is a fourth argument. However, the modern tongues movement does not even measure up to the teaching of this passage; besides, its poor textual support should prevent its use as a prooftext (see chapter V). A fifth argument is that the purpose of the gifts or signs was for the confirmation, not the substitution, of the Word to a pagan world. Since the same conditions prevail today on the mission fields, these sign-gifts are needed there. Actually, this argues against the presence of the sign-gifts in this country because the same conditions do not exist here. Again, it presupposes the reappearance

[31] Roy L. Laurin, *1 Corinthians: Where Life Matures* (Findlay, Ohio: Dunham Publishing Company, 1957), p. 246.
[32] B. F. Cate, *The Nine Gifts of the Spirit Are Not in the Church Today* (Chicago: Regular Baptist Press, 1957), p. 8.
[33] Brumback, *What Meaneth This?, op cit.*, pp. 59-87.

of events which were unique and transitional in Acts (liars struck dead, unsaved blinded, earthquakes opening prison doors, etc.). Sixth, they state that unbelief caused the retrogression of miracles and gifts. However, these gifts were not given in response to faith, but sovereignly as God willed (I Cor. 12:11). Great revivals in church history (e.g., the Reformation) have seen great faith manifested but no miracles or gifts. Their strongest argument is based upon Paul's illustration of a face to face encounter (I Cor. 13:12). Gifts will cease when the believers see Christ. This verse will be discussed more thoroughly later, but at the present time, it will be sufficient to point out that only knowledge of himself is mentioned here, not the gift of tongues.

Gee concluded: "There is nothing in Scripture, reason or experience to make us believe that the gifts are not for today— everyone of them."[34] His conclusion was based upon his interpretation of certain passages (Mark 16:20; cf. Matt. 28:20; Rom. 11:29; Heb. 13:8). The Markan passage has been discussed. It is true that the "gifts and calling of God are without repentance" (Rom. 11:29), but this passage refers to God's calling *of Israel* and His gifts *to Israel* (cf. Rom. 9:4-11). Paul was simply assuring the Roman Christians that God would fulfill all of His promises to Israel (cf. Rom. 11:26). The passage does not refer to the permanence of spiritual gifts; Gee took it out of context. The character and nature of Jesus Christ are the same yesterday, today, and forever (Heb. 13:8), but this does not mean that his program does not change. He once told his disciples not to preach to Gentiles (Matt. 10:5-6); later, He told them to preach to the Gentiles (Matt. 28:18-20). Jesus did not change; *His program* did. This passage cannot be used to support the position that speaking in tongues is valid today because it was done in the apostolic era. To answer Gee, one might say that there is nothing in Scripture, reason, or experience to prove that speaking in tongues is for today.

It must be said, however, that several non-tongues speakers believe that the gifts are permanent and possible today.[35] Lindsell and Woodbridge, former professors at Fuller Seminary, wrote:

> Speaking in tongues, performing "signs," and miraculously healing the sick,—these are possible today, but they are neither necessary nor normal in church life. They are the exception rather than the rule

[34] Gee, *op. cit.*, p. 9.

and should be so regarded. Christians ought not to exalt men who may have these gifts. Nor are those so endowed to become the objects of public adulation.[36]

After denying the existence of the genuine gift of tongues today, Miles admitted: "God can cause you to speak in tongues also in an emergency to communicate with some person who has another language. Our God can do anything."[37] Many non-tongues speakers are reluctant to state that tongues cannot occur today, although they, themselves, do not covet the gift or do not see the necessity of the gift. There are no doubt several reasons for this. Since there is no verse of Scripture that explicitly states that tongues would cease *with the apostolic era*, they leave open the possibility of its occurrence today. In their acceptance of the sovereignty of God, they do not want to impose a limitation upon God's power today. This is commendable and yet, it does not come to grips with the problem of God's purpose for this present age. God could destroy the world today (He has the power), but He will not because it is contrary to His revealed purpose for the church, Israel, and the present world system. Another reason for this position *may* be expediency. Members or leaders of various organizations (ecumenical movement, National Association of Evangelicals, interdenominational schools and mission agencies) must be tolerant of their fellow members who may be tongues speakers.

The third view is that most spiritual gifts, including that of tongues, ended when the canon of the New Testament was completed or when the church of Jesus Christ reached maturity at the end of the apostolic era. Whichever is stated, genuine speaking in tongues ceased by A.D. 100. The gifts which had to do with authority and the giving and discerning of revelation (apostleship, prophecy, miracles, healing, tongues, interpretation of tongues) were temporary, whereas the other gifts were permanent.[38] There are several arguments that give credence to this position.

First, there is the blanket statement that "tongues shall cease" (*glossai pausontai*; 13:8). Speaking in tongues ceased when God no longer gave the gift. That the gift ceased in the apostolic

[35] Edman, *op. cit.*, p. 15. Laurin, *1 Corinthians, op. cit.*, p. 204. Also Norman Grubb, *God Unlimited* (Fort Washington, Penna.: Christian Literature Crusade, n.d.), p. 69. Grubb is a leader in the deeper life movement.
[36] Harold Lindsell and Charles J. Woodbridge, *A Handbook of Christian Truth* (Westwood, N. J.: Fleming H. Revell Company, 1953), p. 322.
[37] Miles, *op. cit.*, p.9.
[38] Walvoord, *op. cit.*, pp. 168-88.

era can be demonstrated by the fact that in the second century and subsequent centuries it did not occur (see chapter II). It would take only one generation without the existence of tongues to pin-point the exact time of ceasing. If the gift were supposed to be permanent, then it would have occurred in *every* generation of *every* century up to the present time. To argue that the gift was active in the apostolic era, then silent for centuries, and is now active again is contrary to the plain statement of Scripture. *When they cease, they cease.* This is a blanket statement—not to be repeated again. To blame its absence upon unbelief is also against the Scriptural teaching of sovereign impartation.

The second argument is that the phrase "that which is perfect" refers to the completed canon which formed the climax of the maturing process of the church. Weaver candidly observed:

> Logically, *to teleion* must refer to completeness or perfection in the *same realm* as that referred to by *to ek merous*. Since *to ek merous* refers to the transmission of divine truth by revelation, the other term *to teleion* must refer to God's *complete* revelation of truth, the entire New Testament (taken of course with its foundational book, the Old Testament).[39]

Prophecy involved the reception and the proclamation of divinely revealed truth. Knowledge involved a revelation of the mind and will of God. No one person received all of the revelation. God revealed Himself to different men at different times imparting progressive truth about Himself and His program (Heb. 1:1). Each Biblical book written only formed a part of the whole. Not until Revelation was written could it be said that God's revelation was complete (*teleion*). This word *teleion* means that something is partially here now, is presently developing, and one day will become complete. This word fits the concept of the progressive revelation of the New Testament of which Paul was aware (John 14: 25-26; 16:12-13; cf. Col. 1:25). These gifts of revelation will cease or be rendered inoperative when revelation is completed. The gift or act of speaking in tongues or prophesying would end, not the content or message of the speaking. The content, divine revelation, was true and no doubt incorporated into the written revelation, the Word of God. Horton, a tongues advocate, admitted

---

[39] Gilbert B. Weaver, " 'Tongues Shall Cease': 1 Corinthians 13:8," Unpublished research paper (Grace Theological Seminary, Winona Lake, Indiana, 1964), p. 12.

that some uses of the gifts contributed to the canon.[40] Although the word *teleios* usually refers to the perfection or maturity of the believer, it is used once of the Scripture (Jas. 1:25). It is used interestingly of the mature church (Eph. 4:13; cf. 2:15) to whom Christ gave gifted leaders for the express purpose of developing the church into maturity (apostles, prophets, evangelists, pastor-teachers). By the time that the apostles, prophets, and evangelists had died, the church was mature with the completed Scriptures in hand and under the leadership of local pastor-teachers, ready to face the non-Christian world without apostolic assistance. If some of the gifts were in existence in the second century (not proved), they may be explained by the fact that the compilation, circulation, and the recognition of canonical books took time. Although the canon was closed, some had an incomplete canon for years.

Paul's two illustrations (13:11-12) serve as a third argument. Progressive development from infancy to maturity in Paul's personal life would best suit the development of the body of Christ (cf. I Cor. 12). There may be a subtle inference here to the gifts of tongues ("spake"), knowledge ("understood"), and prophecy ("thought") which would be "put away" or rendered inoperative by maturity (same word is used: *katargethesetai*, 13:8; cf. *katergeka*, 13:11). Could this be why Paul advanced beyond tongues and wanted only to teach in the church (cf. 14:18-19)? The second illustration is a little more difficult to understand. Weaver argued that it does not refer to the second coming of Christ: "If the mirror [glass] is metaphorical for something, then the "face to face" experience is also metaphorical. If the mirror represents imperfect knowledge, then the face to face encounter is metaphorical for the complete state of knowledge. . . ."[41] This is consistent with the context of partiality and completeness. By looking into the partially revealed Word, man got a partial picture of himself; however, when the Word was completed, then man could see himself exactly as God saw him. Why? Because God had completely revealed the purpose of man and the church in the Word.

Fourth, if the gift of tongues was also a sign to curious Jews (14:21-22), then that significance ended with the destruction of Jerusalem (A.D. 70).

[40] Horton, *Gifts, op. cit.*, p. 72.
[41] Weaver, *op. cit.*, p. 14.

Fifth, in books written after First Corinthians dealing with church problems and normal Christian living, there is no mention of the gift of tongues. The qualifications of elders and deacons do not include any specific gifts (I Tim. 3:1-13; Titus 1:5-9). Christ criticized the seven churches (Rev. 2-3) for many errors of life and doctrine, but there is no mention of tongues. Apparently, these gifts had ceased by this time. Signs, wonders, miracles, and spiritual gifts (Heb. 2:4), in abundance in the early life of the church, passed away as God's purpose for them was withdrawn.

Sixth, Morris regarded the contemporary ignorance of the basic nature of the gifts as an argument against their permanence. He wrote: "But, in view of the fact that they disappeared so speedily and so completely that we do not even know for certain exactly what they were, we must regard them as the gift of God for the time of the church's infancy.[42] Even the Pentecostalists have a problem defining the exact nature of tongues and the gift of interpretation.

Toussaint abridged this third view slightly.[43] He considered the verb differences of 13:8 to be most significant: "Love never faileth (*piptei*): but whether there be prophecies, they shall fail (*katargethesontai*); whether there be tongues, they shall cease (*pausontai*); whether there be knowledge, it shall vanish away (*katargethesetai*)." Whenever the perfect is come, the partial "shall be done away" (*kartargethesetai*). Prophecy and knowledge would be rendered inoperative by Christ's return (*to teleion*), but tongues would cease before this event. Only history could verify the exact point of ceasing. This is based upon the change of verbs (*pauo* for tongues and *katargeo* for prophecy and knowledge). The change of voice is also noted. *Pausontai* is future middle whereas *katargethesetai* is future passive. Two will be rendered inoperative *by* something, whereas tongues will simply cease on its own. The omission of tongues, the key subject of the context, in verses nine and twelve verifies this conclusion. This distinction, contextually and grammatically valid, would destroy the thesis that tongues are permanent. Could it not be that this distinction could be maintained with this one exception. The gifts of prophecy and knowledge would be rendered inoperative by the completion of the canon, whereas

Morris, "Gifts," *op. cit.*, p. 5.
Stanley D. Toussaint, "First Corinthians Thirteen and the Tongues Question." *Bibliotheca Sacra*, CXX (October-December, 1963), 311-16.

tongues would cease before the writing of the last New Testament book. It would be more consistent with the usage of *teleios.*

The gift of tongues, then, must be viewed as a minor gift which was necessary to the infancy of the church but which ceased within God's purpose when God's revelation was completed.

Tongues and Regulations

In his comparison of the gifts of prophecy and tongues (ch. 14), Paul set forth many regulations for the expression of the gift of tongues. Violations of these regulations would reveal that the phenomenon was not divine in origin.

Edification

Paul's main emphasis in this chapter is that all believers in the church should be edified by the exercise of spiritual gifts (14:3,4,5, 6,12,17,19,26,31). Specifically, he admonished them: "Even so ye, forasmuch as ye are zealous of spiritual gifts, seek that ye may excel to the edifying of the church" (14:12) and "Let all things be done unto edifying" (14:26). The exercise of the gift of tongues brought edification to the speaker (14:4); this is fine in itself, but it does not fulfill the true intent of the gifts. A member of the body of Christ was to function in order that the entire body might receive profit. True love for fellow believers does not seek its own edification (13:5) at the expense of the greater edification of the church. Apparently, the Corinthians in their selfish pride and carnality desired this gift more than the others because of its inherent benefits to them, but this attitude was wrong. Paul used his own attitude to correct their thinking (14:17-18):

> I thank my God, I speak with tongues more than ye all:
> Yet in the church I had rather speak five words with my understanding, that by my voice I might teach others also, than ten thousand words in an unknown tongue.

Hoyt commented: "This is a categorical statement that has no exceptions attached to it, and it is almost equivalent to saying that speaking in tongues is practically worthless in the public gathering."[44] The modern movement would reply that Paul is

---

[44] Herman A. Hoyt, "Speaking in Tongues," *Brethren Missionary Herald,* XXV (March 23, 1963), 157.

deprecating only *uninterpreted* tongues, and that tongues plus interpretation does bring edification to the church (cf. 14:5). Since it is possible that no interpretation might be given (14:28), Paul sees little value in the gift of tongues *per se*. In order to be valid, it needed interpretation. But if no interpreter was present, then the person who had the gift of tongues would have to remain silent. Thus, he could not function as a member of the body of Christ to the edification of other believers. Paul desired that they might exercise a gift which would *at all times* minister to edification (12:31; 14:12,39). Even Roberts admitted that "as an instrument of teaching and preaching, tongues are virtually without value."[45]

Interpretation

The regulation of interpretation is clear (14:27-28):

> If any man speak in an unknown tongue, let it be by two, or at the most by three, and that by course; and let one interpret.
> But if there be no interpreter let him keep silence in the church; and let him speak to himself, and to God.

There should be no speaking in tongues without interpretation in the local church. The modern tongues movement has consistently violated this regulation.[46] This passage also teaches that only *one* person (*heis* not *tis*) should interpret regardless of whether there are one, two, or three utterances in tongues. There was to be no interpretation in turn by two or three men. Horton wrongly stated that "one" was not a numeral, but a pronoun. On this basis, he permitted the idea that two, or three interpreters could speak.[47] They therefore violate this regulation also. This passage also teaches that the presence of an interpreter could be known before any speaking in tongues occurred. Believers knew when they had the gift of interpretation, and this fact was recognized by others. However, it is taught that if a person speaks in tongues and no interpretation follows, then the tongue-speaker should pray for an interpretation and give it himself. This concept is based upon 14:15: "Wherefore let him that speaketh in an unknown tongue pray that he may interpret." However, the immediate context (14:1-2) reveals that everyone was speaking in tongues and no one was interpreting. This

---

[45] Roberts, *op. cit.*, p. 94.
[46] See Appendixes I and II. The author has personally observed this several times. It occurs at all times—seeking the baptism, devotional tongues, and the gift of tongues.
[47] Horton, *Gifts*, *op. cit.*, pp. 168-69.

was unprofitable and not edifying. Therefore, Paul admonished the tongue speaker to pray that he might receive the gift of interpretation in order that he might interpret what others were speaking to the edification of the church. Also, if a person could speak in tongues and then pray for the interpretation, what is the sense behind Paul's regulation (14:27-28)? There would always be a potential interpreter present if that were the case. Although a person could have both the gifts of tongues and interpretation, it is unlikely that he exercised both of them on the same occasion. Since the prophets were to be judged by others (*hoi alloi diakrinetosan*; 14: 29), the same procedure would apply to speaking in tongues (14:27). This is also seen in 14:26: "How is it then brethren? when ye come together, every one of you hath a psalm, hath a doctrine, hath a tongue, hath a revelation, hath an interpretation. . . ." Here, a distinction is made between the one who speaks in tongues and the one who interprets. Most interpretations of the modern tongues movement are given either by the speaker himself or by the pastor or leader of the congregation.[48]

Language

It was pointed out earlier (chapter IV) that all speaking in tongues, whether it be the sign of the reception of the Holy Spirit (Acts 2, 10, 19) or the gift of tongues (I Cor. 12–14), was in the form of known languages of the world which could be translated into the language of the congregation. Speaking in gibberish or unknown sounds (these sounds do not manifest the components of known language structure) is foreign to the Biblical accounts of the phenomenon. The modern tongues movement stands indicted because of its frequent and universal violation of this important regulation.

Number and Order

There should be no more than three individual instances of speaking in tongues in one service, and they should occur one at a time, not simultaneously (14:27). Simultaneous speaking in tongues by many only leads to mass confusion and ridicule by unbelievers (14:23). And yet, this is done by the modern tongues movement *with approval*. In reference to singing in tongues ("sing

[48] See Appendixes I and II for illustrations.

with the spirit" is its synonym according to them; 14:15), Brumback observed: "We have heard this singing in tongues often by a
whole congregation, occasionally by a smaller group and even by
a single believer. . . ."[49] Simultaneous occurrences of the gift of
tongues, whether in the form of speaking, praying, or singing, are
condemned by Paul. Pentecostalists admit the distinction between
tongues in Acts (evidential) and tongues in Corinth (gift); therefore the simultaneous occurrences in Acts cannot be used to support
their usage of the simultaneous occurences of the gift.

At all times, public speakers, whether they be speakers in
tongues or prophets, should manifest restraint and self-control in
the exercise of their gifts (14:28,29,30,32; cf. Gal. 5:22-23—Fruit
of the Spirit is . . . self-control). God is not the author of confusion
but of peace (14:33). He does everything decently and in order
(14:40). Therefore, any speaking in tongues in the atmosphere of
confusion is not of God.[50] Genuine speaking in tongues will follow
the regulations set forth in the Word of God.

Sex

> Let your women keep silence in the churches: for it is not
> permitted unto them to speak; but they are commanded to be under
> obedience, as also saith the law.
> And if they will learn anything, let them ask their husbands at
> home, for it is a shame for women to speak in the church (14:34-35).

In what area is a woman not permitted to speak in a local church
service? Horton, a Pentecostalist, said that women should not speak
in judging the prophets (14:29) or in asking questions in order to
learn (14:35).[51] According to him and the modern tongues movement, this prohibition of women does not refer to speaking in tongues
or prophesying. He admitted that all movements that have women
for their heads or leaders teach error, and yet, many Pentecostal
denominations and churches have had women as leaders or pastors
(e.g., Aimee Semple McPherson) and the modern movement is no
exception (e.g., Jean Stone). Brumback called this passage and
First Timothy 2:11-12 a general rule, rather than an absolute rule
which will admit no exceptions.[52] However, since Paul does not
permit any exceptions, why should we?

---

[49] Brumback, *What Meaneth This?*, op. cit., p. 294. Also see Appendix I for an
illustration of two speaking in tongues at the same time.
[50] See Appendixes I and II for illustrations of confusion.
[51] Horton, *Gifts*, op. cit., p. 207.
[52] Brumback, *What Meaneth This?*, op. cit., p. 314.

Apart from the question of prophecy, many believe that this is a prohibition against speaking in tongues by women.[53] The prohibition to speak uses the same word (*laleo*) as was used of speaking in tongues (14:34-35; cf. 14:27-28). The passage is still in the context of speaking in tongues (cf. 14:37, *pneumatikos,* a synonym for tongue speaker, and 14:39); therefore it need not be limited to judging or asking questions. If Paul were only referring to judging or asking questions, he could have and would have used those words (*diakrino,* 14:29, and *eperotao,* 14:35) to point out his exact meaning.

Some have included prophecy in this prohibition. Grosheide said that women were allowed to prophesy but not when the congregation officially met.[54] Parry excluded prophecy wherever it took place.[55] Although Paul mentioned prophecy and women earlier (I Cor. 11:2-16), he was basically dealing with the issue of the veiling of women and their insubordination. In this chapter (ch. 14), Paul even forbade women from prophesying. This word *laleo* is also used of prophetic speaking (14:29), so prophecy may be included in the prohibition. If not, certainly speaking in tongues by women is what Paul meant. This regulation alone would show that the modern tongues movement is not Biblical.

Sign to Unbelievers

> In the law it is written, With men of other tongues and other lips will I speak unto this people; and yet for all that will they not hear me, saith the Lord.
> Wherefore tongues are for a sign, not to them that believe, but to them that believe not: but prophesying serveth not for them that believe not, but for them which believe (14:21-22).

Apart from the edification to the church through interpretation, the gift of tongues served as a sign to unbelievers, especially and possibly exclusively Jewish unbelievers. Because of the reference to "this people" (Israel) and the usage of the inferential conjunction "wherefore" (*hoste*), Hodges believed that the true intent of tongues was to be seen in the Old Testament quotation (14:21; cf. Isa. 28:11-12). He wrote: "Tongues were given as a sign to the Jewish

---

[53] M. R. DeHaan, *Holy Spirit Baptism* (Grand Rapids: Radio Bible Class, 1964), pp. 31-32.
[54] F. W. Grosheide, *Commentary on the First Epistle to the Corinthians* (Grand Rapids: Wm. B. Eerdmans Publishing Co., 1953), p. 341.
[55] R. St. John Parry (ed.), *The First Epistle of Paul the Apostle to the Corinthians* (Cambridge: Cambridge University Press, 1916), pp. 210-11.

people only, from which it follows that the average heathen visitor to the Christian assembly (far more likely to be a Gentile than a hostile Jew) would be exposed to a phenomenon never intended for him in the first place."[56] The context (14:21-22; cf. 1:22: "Jews require a sign") and the first occurrence of tongues (Acts 2:1-13) would support this conclusion. However, Paul may just be using the passage to show that tongues is a sign to unbelievers who will remain unconvinced and firm in their unbelief. The gift of tongues was not used to proclaim the gospel to the unsaved. Such claims by the modern tongues movement (there are many) as to this purpose must be regarded as contrary to the Biblical significance.

Reception

Horton wrote: "It is the Lord's expressed desire that *all* should speak with tongues (I Cor. 14:5). . . . If you have never thus spoken, seek the Spirit until you do."[57] Is this true? No. Paul's desire (14:5) would not be any more fulfilled than his desire to be accursed for the sake of Israel (Rom. 9:3). The latter was impossible because of God's elective purpose (Rom. 8:28-39), and the former desire was impossible because of the nature of the body of Christ. All members do not have the same gift. Paul pointed this out clearly: "Do all speak with tongues?" (12:30). The expected answer is no. Would the Holy Spirit cause a believer to covet the least gift (tongues) when Paul told the Corinthians to covet the best gifts (12:31; 14:1,39)? No! It must be remembered that no matter how much a person prays or covets a gift, it is still a *gift* and is only sovereignly given (*as He will*). The appeal of Paul is also to the church as a whole. They should desire that the best gifts be manifested in their midst, not that each Christian who has a gift should desire others.

Prohibition

In conclusion, Paul wrote: "Wherefore, brethren, covet to prophesy, and forbid not to speak with tongues" (14:39). The modern tongues movement has seized upon this verse as a warning against suppression of the manifestations of the spiritual gifts. Brumback stated: "Why did the Holy Spirit inspire him to express

---

[56] Hodges, *op. cit.*, p. 231.
[57] Horton, *Gifts, op. cit.*, p. 156.

this command in negative? Because He knew that there would be need for a strong deterrent to the divers and sundry efforts to exclude tongues not only at Corinth but also throughout church history."[58] However, Paul did not tell the Corinthians to covet tongues either! Since the gift of tongues was then in existence, neither he nor the Corinthians would forbid its usage. However, they could regulate its manifestation. This verse can't be used to prove that tongues must be permitted today. Only the purpose of God for today will reveal whether it *will* happen today.

The regulations of tongues are many. This very fact shows that the phenomenon was either misused or simulated often and easily. This may serve as another reason why tongues were only meant to be temporary. As to regulations and the present movement, Hoyt concluded: "It is very possible that rigid application would completely eliminate their employment."[59] Personal study and observation by the author would confirm this conclusion.

Acts vs. First Corinthians

Are the tongues in Acts and in First Corinthians of the same character and for the same purpose? Or, do they have a different character and purpose? Or, do they have the same character but a different purpose?

Ruble believed that the various occurrences had the same character and purpose. He wrote:

> The explanation of the differences between tongues in Acts and tongues in I Corinthians centers around the concepts of progressive revelation and dispensational distinctives. The glossolalia in Acts occurred some years before that in I Corinthians. It would be expected that with the passage of years regulations would be set up in the churches to govern the use of the spiritual gifts.[60]

However, the last occurrence of tongues in Acts (19:1-7) took place during Paul's third journey in Ephesus. At this time Paul wrote First Corinthians from Ephesus; therefore, it would be more logical to conclude that the Corinthian manifestation of tongues preceded that of the disciples of John the Baptist, although the Corinthian letter was written shortly after the Ephesian occurrence. Thus, if regulations were imposed, they were done so quickly, not progress-

---

[58] Brumback, *What Meaneth This?*, *op. cit.*, p. 172.
[59] Hoyt, *op. cit.* (April 20, 1963), p. 206.
[60] Ruble, *op. cit.*, pp. 131-32.

ively. Even Gee, a Pentecostalist, admitted the continuity and the progressive regulation of the experience from Acts to First Corinthians.[61]

However, the study of these two books has demonstrated that the phenomenon of tongues in both was the same in character but different in purpose. MacDonald admitted this.[62] Both consisted of speaking in known languages and of magnifying God. Both were spoken by men under the control of the Holy Spirit and both had significance as signs. Here, the similarity stops. In Acts, speaking in tongues was a transitional sign of the unique reception of the Holy Spirit by four different classes of people. In First Corinthians, tongues was a spiritual gift given to some believers for the edification of the church. Regulations of the gift of tongues (number, in order, need of interpreter, etc.) are not seen in the Acts occurrences. Because of this difference in purpose, Brumback argued:

> If there is a clear distinction between the tongues phenomenon in Acts and that in I Corinthians, then the Pentecostal argument for tongues as the initial, physical evidence is well-nigh irrefutable. If not, then the Pentecostal theology on the evidence teaching suffers a severe blow. This is, perhaps, the decisive point of the entire controversy.[63]

There is a difference of purpose, but the Pentecostal definition of purpose is wrong. In Acts, tongues were not the initial, physical sign of the baptism in the Holy Spirit (which they have wrongly defined). Admission of a difference in purpose does not mean that the Pentecostal position is irrefutable. Study of the phenomena and their distinctive purposes in Acts and in Corinthians has shown that these purposes no longer exist; therefore genuine tongues do not occur today. Many attempts to refute Pentecostalism have been based upon the proposition that the phenomena were the same in character and in purpose. These men would point out that not all speak in tongues (I Cor. 12:30), and yet all have been baptized in the Holy Spirit (I Cor. 12:13); therefore, tongues is not an evidence of the baptism in the Holy Spirit. However, it is not necessary to maintain sameness in character and in purpose in order to refute the doctrinal basis of the modern tongues movement. The doctrinal

---

[61] Gee, *op. cit.*, p. 57.
[62] William G. MacDonald, "Glossolalia in the New Testament," *Bulletin of the Evangelical Theological Society*, VII (Spring, 1964), 65. Reprinted in booklet form by Gospel Publishing House, Springfield, Mo.
[63] Brumback, *What Meaneth This?*, *op. cit.*, pp. 261-62.

basis and the personal experiences of tongues advocates do not harmonize with the characteristics of the two different purposes.

The modern tongues movement admits to three different types of tongues. First, a person will speak in tongues as the initial, physical evidence of the baptism in the Holy Spirit (Acts 2, 8, 10, 19). Second, a person who has had this experience can continue to speak in simple tongues for private devotions (without need of interpretation) for self-edification. Third, to some God gives the gift of tongues which must be exercised in the local church attended by the gift of interpretation. The first type has been proved to be false. The distinction between the second and the third was made arbitrarily from First Corinthians. MacDonald classified the verses as denoting personal use (14:6,9,16,18,23,26,28), church use (12:10,28,30; 14:5b,13,27,39), and both uses (13:1,8; 14:2, 4,5a,14,15,22).[64] This distinction has been imposed upon this passage which deals strictly with spiritual gifts to be exercised in the local church for the edification of all. It has been set forth as a justification for uninterpreted tongues in private and in public.[65] The gift of tongues was a valid use in the infant church period, but its manifestation is no longer needed today.

Thus, the tongues in Acts and in First Corinthians were of two types. They were the same in essential character, but different in purpose.

---

[64] MacDonald, *op. cit.*, pp. 63-65.
[65] See Appendix I for illustrations.

CHAPTER VIII

CONCLUSION

"Throughout the history of the church, no spiritual gift has occasioned so much continual controversy as the gift of tongues."[1] We have demonstrated the truth of that observation. The modern tongues movement has increased this controversy and has stimulated much research on the phenomenon of tongues. We have attempted to evaluate this movement in the light of the Scriptures.

It was first seen that the phenomenon of ecstatic speech or tongues was not unique to Biblical Christianity, but that it was also found in pagan religions. This demonstrated that ecstatic speech could be Satanically or artificially produced. No occurrences of tongues were seen in the Old Testament. In the apostolic era, the Biblical phenomenon first occurred (Acts 2, 10, 19; I Cor. 12–14). No genuine manifestations of tongues were seen in the post-apostolic period through the Protestant Reformation. In the next three centuries, perverted manifestations of tongues occurred among heretical groups of different doctrinal persuasion. Modern Pentecostalism is a twentieth century movement with its basis in Arminian, holiness theology. It is this movement that has claimed the recovery of the phenomenon of tongues and that has penetrated the historic denominations in the past decade. Therefore there is no historical continuity of the phenomenon of tongues from the Biblical era to the present situation. Tongues did indeed cease!

The current tongues movement is being pushed chiefly by the Full Gospel Business Men's Fellowship International and other related groups, such as the Blessed Trinity Society. All of the major denominations have been penetrated and influenced by this new emphasis. The movement is characterized by all types of phenomena—tongues, healings, visions, dreams, direct revelation, etc. These experiences are contrary to the Biblical pattern of true spiritual experiences. Although the movement claims to be of divine

---

[1] Walvoord, *op. cit.*, p. 180.

origin, its phenomena are best explained by Satanic origin, psychologically produced, or artificially simulated. In most cases, it appears to be a human effort to recreate or simulate a transitional Biblical phenomenon.

The true nature of Biblical glossolalia was that known, foreign languages were spoken by a believer who had never learned them and who was controlled by the Holy Spirit. The modern tongues movement claims that tongue speaking can be in either known languages or unknown sounds, with the latter being spoken much more than the former. Since speaking in unknown sounds is unscriptural, the modern movement has not recovered the Biblical phenomenon.

The modern tongues movement claims that as long as the great commission is carried out, speaking in tongues will occur (Mark 16:15-20). True faith in God will cause the phenomenon to appear in the individual's life. However, the faith mentioned in this passage is faith for salvation, not faith to receive a gift. Actually, the passage teaches that everyone who believes in Christ *will* speak in tongues. This is contrary to the experiences of past generations of believers and of the modern movement itself. Since the passage has poor textual authenticity, it should not be used to prove any position.

The modern movement also claims that speaking in tongues was the initial, physical evidence of the baptism of the Holy Spirit (Acts 2, 8, 10, 19). However, they have misunderstood the Biblical doctrine of the baptism of the Holy Spirit and the transitional nature of the Book of Acts. Speaking in tongues was the sign of the initial introduction of the Holy Spirit's ministry to four different classes of people (Jews, Samaritans[?], Gentiles, disciples of John the Baptist). It occurred then and only then for that particular purpose. These occurrences were never intended to become a pattern for the reception of the Spirit by subsequent believers. Thy could not because no two of the four are the same. Actually, the experiences of many Pentecostalists are contrary to their own formulated pattern.

The modern tongues movement claims that the spiritual gifts, including the gift of tongues, were intended by God to become a permanent part of church life and history. However, many of these gifts (including tongues) were temporary, designed to be used by the infant church until the New Testament canon and revelation were closed and the church was mature as the result of the apostolic, prophetic ministry. It was clearly stated that the gift of tongues would cease, and church history revealed that it did in the first century. The inward (love) and the outward regulations of the gift of tongues are not practiced by the modern tongues movement. It claims that the forbidding of tongues today is anti-Scriptural (I Cor. 14:39) and a limitation upon the sovereign will of God. However, the question is not whether God *can* give the gift of tongues today; it is whether God has purposed to do so. As Walvoord wrote:

> It is, of course, impossible for anyone to prove experimentally that speaking in tongues cannot occur today. It may be demonstrated, however, that speaking in tongues is not essential to God's purpose now, and that there are good reasons to believe that most if not all the phenomena which are advanced as proof of modern speaking in tongues is either psychological or demonic activity.[2]

What, then, is the modern tongues movement? First, it is the penetration and the presence of the old Pentecostalism within churches of historic Protestantism. Although they may claim to be Presbyterians or Baptists with a Pentecostal experience, in actuality they are now Pentecostalists holding membership in Presbyterian or Baptist churches. They support Pentecostal preachers (e.g., Oral Roberts), publications, and schools (e.g., Oral Roberts University) and find their best fellowship within the Full Gospel Business Men's Fellowship program. The charismatic movement within the historic churches is not a spontaneous movement from within, but rather an active recruitment from without.

Second, the modern tongues movement is an essential part of the ecumenical atmosphere. One key leader, Harold Bredesen, affirmed: "Today this living, uncontrollable Spirit is sovereignly at work in the Roman Catholic Church and among Protestants, both liberal and conservative."[3] A Lutheran minister and tongues speaker wrote:

> I have been having dialogues with Catholics and with Pentecostals and it has been a wonderful blessing. In Brooklyn we have two dialogue groups now, composed of Lutheran ministers of all flavors and young Roman Catholic priests. We meet and study the Scriptures together, pray together, talk about community problems, and discuss mutual involvement of our parishes.
> Recently I attended a Roman Catholic, Episcopalian and Lutheran retreat. The Holy Spirit is moving in the Roman Catholic Church. *I am convinced that the basic meaning of the Charismatic Renewal*

[2] *Ibid.,* pp. 185-186.

is the reunion of the churches. Not a reunion of compromise, of the creation of a super-church, but a renovation as to what the unity of the Spirit means.[4] (Italics mine).

Whether all Pentecostal leaders support these claims is beside the point. It is a fact that this significance of the modern tongues movement is so stated by some of their own leaders. Liberals, conservatives, Protestants, and Catholics are being drawn together by the phenomenon of speaking in tongues. This *may* supply the inner unity that the ecumenical movement could not do organizationally. It is an inner unity based upon experience, not doctrine.

Third, the modern tongues movement reflects a confusion and ignorance of Biblical doctrine. It has its basis in Arminianism and in spiritual immaturity. Many of their experiences simulate the crisis encounter of Barthian neo-orthodoxy. All kinds of doctrinal foundations are acceped by them as long as the person has had the proper experience. Note the published testimonies by Roman Catholics (sacramentalism), Church of Christ (baptismal regeneration), Arminians, and liberals. Their emphasis upon extra-Biblical revelation and phenomena (visions, dreams, healings, tongues) is unhealthy and contrary to the witness of the Holy Spirit through the Word.. Their doctrinal concepts of the baptism of the Holy Spirit and the "latter rain" fulfillment must be rejected.

Fourth, the modern tongues movement is based upon experience, not doctrine. Someone once penned the maxim: "The man who has an experience is never at the mercy of a man who has an argument." This is true to a certain extent, but a religious experience in itself can never be the final test of its genuineness. The Bible must forever be the basis of faith and practice. It must always judge experiences to determine their validity. Walvoord pointed out the errors of doctrine based upon experience:

> Experience ever possesses two fatal grounds for error: (1) a misapprehension of the experience itself in its content and divine origin; (2) a faulty conclusion as to the doctrinal meaning of the experience. Hence, on the one hand, an experience supposedly of divine origin may be purely psychological, or worse, a deceiving device of Satan himself. On the other hand, a genuine experience may be misunderstood and mislabeled, as the common denomination of the work of the filling of the Spirit as the baptism of the Spirit.[5]

[3] Harold Bredesen, "Return to the Charismata," *Trinity*, II (Whitsuntide, 1962), 22.
[4] Erwin Prange, "A New Ministry," *Full Gospel Busines Men's Voice*, XIII (April, 1965), 7.
[5] Walvoord, *op. cit.*, p. 174.

The modern tongues movement is guilty of both of these errors.

We conclude by quoting Paul, who said: "Tongues shall cease" (I Cor. 13:8). They have.

APPENDIX I

The author attended a monthly banquet of the Full Gospel Men's Fellowship International (FGBMFI) in Dayton, Ohio, at the Stratford House on May 21, 1965. This banquet was attended by about sixty people, equally divided between men and women. At least four denominations (Baptist, Methodist, Presbyterian, and Pentecostal) were represented.

The banquet began with group singing and special music. After the dinner, announcements of coming meetings were given. Testimonies of healing followed. One woman claimed that she had been healed of a painful foot ailment. One morning she awoke with this pain in her foot, could not put her shoe on, and had to limp. She prayed and she had others pray for her, but the pain did not go away. From that point, whenever she felt the pain in her foot, she said within herself: "Thank you, Lord, for taking away the pain." The pain persisted throughout the day, but finally went away in the evening, and did not return since that time. This type of healing is typical of many of the Pentecostal claims to healing. It is a progressive type, far different from the instantaneous type mentioned in the Bible. It is no different in character than that which has been experienced by non-Pentecostal Christians who believe that God can and does heal, but who also believe that faith healers and the gift of healing are not for today. This testimony smacked of the "mind over matter" technique.

The speaker for the evening was Rev. Robert P. Durand, minister of the Dilworthtown Presbyterian Church in West Chester, Pennsylvania. He said that he was saved, received the baptism of the Holy Spirit, spoke with tongues, and was healed of constant stuttering under the ministry of James Brown, a Presbyterian tongues-speaker. Although his speech was good, elements of stuttering were still present. Oftentimes, the beginning of a word or phrase was repeated two or three times before it was finally spoken clearly. In his message, Durand claimed that the fulfillment of the vision of dry bones (Ezekiel 37) was to be seen in the charismatic revival among the historic, denominational churches. However, this prophecy refers only to the "whole house of Israel" (Ezek. 37:11) and to the time when God will restore Israel to the land of Palestine.

After the message, the people stood and began to pray and to praise God with uplifted hands. A woman (about ten feet away and facing me) began to utter strange sounds, quietly but audibly. They had a dental quality and sounded like "Tica-Tica-Tica," repeated rapidly. She did this for a while, then suddenly spoke the same sounds very loudly. A hush came over the group as she uttered these sounds for about a minute. When she stopped, Durand asked for an interpretation. There was silence for a minute, then Durand, himself, began to give an interpretation. In this, he quoted the Messianic prophecy which Jesus read and referred to Himself in the synagogue at Nazareth (Isa. 61:1; cf. Luke 4:16-21). Durand proceeded to apply this prophecy to each person in attendance at the banquet. When he stopped, bedlam broke loose. Shouts of praise echoed throughout the room because God had spoken directly to them. The previously mentioned woman again began to utter the same sounds audibly. A teen-aged boy (two seats down) began to utter three or four syllables over and over. There was no attempt to gain an interpretation for this speaking.

When the people quieted down, Durand asked that two lines be formed—one for receiving the baptism of the Holy Spirit and one for healing. Durand then came back to where I was standing, talked to a teen-aged boy standing next to me (Jay Thatcher), and took him forward to the pulpit area. I followed in order to observe what would happen. Durand then had Thatcher sit down and raise his arms. Thatcher's friend (the boy who uttered three or four syllables before) grasped his one hand. Durand made the mark of the cross on Thatcher's forehead, laid his one hand upon Thatcher's head, and grasped the shoulder with the other. Durand told Thatcher that he could receive the baptism of the Holy Spirit if he would only believe. He told Thatcher to repeat the phrase "monee-monee-monee" over and over until he began speaking in tongues. While Thatcher was doing this, Durand spoke a phrase of unknown syllables which seemingly were repeated by Thatcher (actually hard to tell for sure). Durand then grabbed his shoulders and shouted that Thatcher had received the baptism. Later, he instructed the boy that he had received the experience and that he should not permit anyone to tell him that he had not done so.

During the time that Durand was dealing with Thatcher, many people were urging Thatcher on with shouts of exhortations. Also, the same woman, who was in the healing line, was uttering her familiar phrase "Tica-tica-tica" over and over, again without interpretation.

The boy who had spoken in tongues earlier told Durand that he wanted something more, namely the gift of prophecy. However, Durand advised him to seek love, not certain gifts. Durand then laid hands on an elderly woman who desired relief from a headache. In the back of the room, a boy was lying on his stomach on the floor, groaning and sobbing. I found out from his father that his boy was in a terrible backslidden condition and was under a great burden of sin. During this after-service, people were just milling around— talking, drinking coffee, leaving and entering the room. When I left the room, the meeting was still going on (already three hours in duration).

A few observations are in order. There were false interpretations and applications in both the message and the interpretation of tongue-speaking by Durand. His claim to healing from stuttering was not altogether authenticated by his speech. Some audible speaking in tongues was left uninterpreted, which is contrary to Paul's directives (I Cor. 14:28). Instructions to speak in tongues are contrary to the Biblical examples. I got the impression that most of these people were sincere in their efforts to recreate the Biblical events but that their immaturity caused them to err and to identify error as truth. This must be expected from a human effort to reconstruct that which was performed by the Holy Spirit.

APPENDIX II

The author attended a Sunday evening service at the First Pentecostal Church, Xenia, Ohio, on May 30, 1965. In a personal conversation, this church had been characterized as "too emotional" by a minister of the Assemblies of God. These personal observations will confirm this evaluation.

There were several altar calls even before the message was given. During one of these, one woman had hands laid upon her for healing. There was much shouting and foot-stomping, but there was no claim or outward evidence of healing.

Throughout the preliminaries of the service (singing, prayer, short exhortations), women would stand to their feet and start shaking. Their heads would snap backward and forward, increasing in speed and then decreasing. Many would lean their bodies backward with arms raised. I actually expected some of them to fall to the floor from this position, but none did. One woman went to the front of the auditorium and went through these body motions as she walked back and forth. Another left her seat and started dancing a jig in the aisle. She danced to the back of the church, swinging her arms back and forth. At the back, her hand hit her husband who then went forward when the pastor exhorted him to make things right with the Lord. Some of these women also spoke words, but they could not be discerned because of the distance between them and me. If they were speaking in tongues, there was no attempt to gain an interpretation.

At one point in the service, three men left the choir and started running up and down the aisles. They were joined by a young man who left his seat in the pew and ran after them. They made about three circuits of the church and returned to their respective seats. No explanation of their conduct was given. Before the sermon, one of these men stood on the pew in the choir and spoke in tongues for several minutes. Without any delay or hesitation, he followed with an interpretation, basically exhorting the people to live for the Lord and to listen to the preacher.

The pastor's physical actions during his message were just as uncontrolled. He walked and ran all over the platform, preached in the aisles and stood on the pews. His message was disconnected. I received the impression that he said whatever came into his mind and that he had said many of these things before. The service was certainly not conducted "decently and in order" (I Cor. 14:40).

APPENDIX III

Raymond Frame, a former missionary to China, attended a Chinese Pentecostal service in which there was a definite appeal to receive the baptism of the Holy Spirit accompanied by the physical evidence of speaking in tongues. During his attempt to receive this experience, Frame came to the conclusion that the power of Satan, not of God, was operating in his life. Here is his complete testimony:

> However, when one of my missionary associates standing beside me suddenly became agitated and began shouting loudly in excellent Chinese, leaping and waving his arms and obviously under the control of a power quite beyond himself, my resistance weakened. I didn't want to be left out of the blessing that he was receiving. I let my mind become quite blank and began yielding myself to the external power outside myself that seemed to be pleading for full control of me.
>
> At once a feeling of paralysis began to numb my feet. It soon affected my legs. I knew that before long I too would be lying helplessly on the floor as were several others in the crowd. At the instant the numbness reached my knees, I became alarmed. "This thing is coming upon me, not from heaven, but from beneath. This is the wrong direction," I thought to myself. Without a moment's hesitation, I cried out, "May the blood of Christ protect me from this thing!"
>
> At once it vanished and I was normal again.
>
> A month later I met that co-worker of mine at another place. He appeared to be a sober and chastened man. "You know, Ray, that thing that happened to me that night wasn't of God. It was of the devil."
>
> . . . my friend then described the spiritual darkness into which he was plunged, following that ecstatic experience.[1]

[1] Raymond Frame, "Something Unusual," *His*, XXIV (December, 1963), 27.

BIBLIOGRAPHY

A. BOOKS

Abbott-Smith, G. *A Manual Greek Lexicon of the New Testament.* Edinburgh: T. & Clark, 1954.

Alford, Henry. *The Greek Testament.* 4 vols. London: Longmans, Green, and Co., 1894.

Arndt, William F., and Gingrich, F. Wilbur. *A Greek-English Lexicon of the New Testament.* Chicago: The University of Chicago Press, 1957.

Barclay, William. *The Letters to the Corinthians.* Philadelphia: The Westminster Press, 1956.

Barton, George A. *Archeology and the Bible.* Philadelphia: American Sunday School Union, 1916.

Bauman, Louis S. *The Tongues Movement.* Winona Lake, Ind.: The Brethren Missionary Herald Co., reprinted 1963.

Blaiklock, E. M. *The Acts of the Apostles.* Grand Rapids: Wm. B. Eerdmans Publishing Company, 1959.

Bruce, F. F. *Commentary on the Book of the Acts.* Grand Rapids: Wm. B. Eerdmans Publishing Company, 1954.

Brumback, Carl. *Suddenly From Heaven.* Springfield, Mo.: Gospel Publishing House, 1961.

————. *"What Meaneth This?"* Springfield, Mo.: The Gospel Publishing House, 1947.

Buttrick, George Arthur (ed.). *The Interpreter's Bible.* 12 vols. New York: Abingdon-Cokesbury Press, 1953.

Cate, B. F. *The Nine Gifts of the Spirit Are Not in the Church Today.* Chicago: Regular Baptist Press, 1957.

Cole, R. A. *The Gospel According to St. Mark.* Grand Rapids: Wm. B. Eerdmans Publishing Company, 1961.

Cross, F. L. (ed.) *The Oxford Dictionary of the Christian Church.* London: Oxford University Press, 1958.

Dalton, Robert Chandler. *Tongues Like as of Fire.* Springfield, Mo.: The Gospel Publishing House, 1945.

Dana, H. E. and Mantey, Julius R. *A Manual Grammer of the Greek New Testament.* New York. The Macmillan Company, 1953.

Davidson, F. (ed.) *The New Bible Commentary.* Grand Rapids: Wm. B. Eerdmans Publishing Company, 1953.

De Haan, M. R. *Holy Spirit Baptism.* Grand Rapids: Radio Bible Class, 1964.

Douglas, J. D. (ed.) *The New Bible Dictionary.* Grand Rapids: Wm. B. Eerdmans Publishing Company, 1962.

Frodsham, Stanley Howard. *With Signs Following.* Springfield, Mo.: Gospel Publishing House, 1946.

Gaebelein, Arno C. *The Annotated Bible.* 9 vols. New York: Our Hope, 1916.

Gee, Donald. *Concerning Spiritual Gifts.* Springfield, Missouri: The Gospel Publishing House, n.d.

Godet, F. *Commentary on the First Epistle of St. Paul to the Corinthians.* 2 vols. Trans. A Cusin. Grand Rapids: Zondervan Publishing House, 1957.

Gould, Ezra P. *A Critical and Exegetical Commentary on the Gospel According to St. Mark.* New York: Charles Scribner's Sons, 1913.

Grosheide, F. W. *Commentary on the First Epistle to the Corinthians.* Grand Rapids: Wm. B. Eerdmans Publishing Company, 1953.

Grubb, Norman. *God Unlimited.* Fort Washington, Penna.: Christian Literature Crusade, n.d.

Harrison, Everett F. *Introduction to the New Testament.* Grand Rapids: Wm. B. Eerdmans Publishing Company, 1964.

Hillis, Don W. *What Can Tongues Do For You?* Chicago: Moody Press, 1963.

Hodge, Charles. *An Exposition of the First Epistle to the Corinthians.* Grand Rapids: Wm. B. Eerdmans Publishing Company, 1950.

Horton, Harold. *The Gifts of the Spirit.* Bedfordshire, England: Redemption Tidings Bookroom, 1946.

————. *What is the Good of Speaking with Tongues?* London: Assemblies of God Publishing House, 1960.

Ironside, H. A. *Addresses on the First Epistle to the Corinthians.* New York: Loizeaux Brothers, 1955.

————. *Holiness, the False and the True.* New York: Loizeaux Brothers, 1947.

Jamieson, Robert, Fausett, A. R., and Brown, David. *A Commentary, Critical and Explanatory on the Old and New Testaments.* Grand Rapids: Zondervan Publishing House, n.d.

Jensen, Jerry (ed.) *Attorneys' Evidence on the Baptism in the Holy Spirit.* Los Angeles: Full Gospel Business Men's Fellowship International, 1965.

————. *Baptists and the Baptism of the Holy Spirit.* Los Angeles: Full Gospel Business Men's Fellowship International, 1963.

————. *Episcopalians and the Baptism in the Holy Spirit.* Los Angeles: Full Gopel Business Men's Fellowship International, 1964.

————. *Methodists and the Baptism of the Holy Spirit.* Los Angeles: Full Gospel Business Men's Fellowship International, 1963.

————. *Presbyterians and the Baptism of the Holy Spirit.* Los Angeles: Full Gospel Business Men's Fellowship International, 1963.

Joy, Donald M. *The Holy Spirit and You.* Winona Lake: Light and Life Press, 1965.

Kelsey, Morton T. *Tongue Speaking.* Garden City, N. Y.: Doubleday & Company, Inc., 1964.

Kendrick, Klaude. *The Promise Fulfilled.* Springfield, Missouri: Gospel Publishing House, 1961.

Kittel, Gerhard (ed.) *Theological Dictionary of the New Testament.* Vol. I. Translated by Geoffrey W. Bromiley. Grand Rapids: Wm. B. Eerdmans Publishing Company, 1964.

Kuyper, Abraham. *The Work of the Holy Spirit.* New York: Funk & Wagnalls Company, 1900.

Landis, Benson Y. *Yearbook of American Churches.* New York: National Council of the Churches of Christ in the U. S. A., 1965.

Laurin, Roy L. *Acts: Life in Action.* Findlay, Ohio: Dunham Publishing Company, 1962.

————. *1 Corinthians: Where Life Matures.* Findlay, Ohio: Dunham Publishing Company, 1957.

Lenski, R. C. H. *The Interpretation of St. Paul's First and Second Epistle to the Corinthians.* Columbus, Ohio: Wartburg Press, 1957.

————. *The Interpretation of The Acts of the Apostles.* Columbus, Ohio: The Wartburg Press, 1957.

Lightner, Robert P. *Speaking in Tongues and Divine Healing.* Des Plaines, Illinois: Regular Baptist Press, 1965.

Lindsell, Harold, and Woodbridge, Charles J. *A Handbook of Christian Truth.* Westwood, N. J.: Fleming H. Revell Company, 1953.

Mac Donald, William G. *Glossolalia in the New Testament.* Springfield, Mo.: Gcspel Publishing House, n.d.

Martin, Ira J., 3rd. *Glossolalia in the Apostolic Church*. Berea, Ky.: Berea College Press, 1960.

Metz, Donald S. *Speaking in Tongues*. Kansas City, Mo.: Nazarene Publishing House, 1964.

Meyer, Heinrich August Wilhelm. *Critical and Exegetical Handbooks to the Acts of the Apostles*. New York: Funk & Wagnalls, 1889.

Morgan, G. Campbell. *The Acts of the Apostles*. New York: Fleming H. Revell Company, 1924.

Morgan, G. Campbell. *The Spirit of God*. New York: Fleming H. Revell Company, 1900.

Morris, Leon. *The First Epistle of Paul to the Corinthians*. Grand Rapids: Wm. B. Eerdmans Publishing Company, 1958.

Moulton, James Hope and Milligan, George. *The Vocabulary of the Greek Testament*. Grand Rapids: Wm. B. Eerdmans Publishing Company, 1963.

Nickel, Thomas R. *The Shakarian Story*. Los Angeles: Full Gospel Business Men's Fellowship International, 1964.

Pache, Rene. *The Person and Work of the Holy Spirit*. Chicago: Moody Press, 1954.

Palmer, Edwin H. *The Holy Spirit*. Philadelphia: Presbyterian and Reformed Publishing Company, 1962.

Parry, R. St. John (ed.). *The First Epistle of Paul the Apostle to the Corinthians*. Cambridge: Cambridge University Press, 1916.

Payne, J. Barton. *The Imminent Appearing of Christ*. Grand Rapids: Wm. B. Eerdmans Publishing Company, 1962.

Rackham, Richard Belward. *The Acts of the Apostles*. London: Methuen & Co. Ltd., 1953.

Ramm, Bernard. *The Witness of the Spirit*. Grand Rapids: Wm. B. Eerdmans Publishing Company, 1960.

Roberts, Oral. *The Baptism with the Holy Spirit and the value of speaking in tongues today*. Tulsa: Oklahoma: By the author, 1964.

Robertson, Archibold, and Plummer, Alfred. *A Critical and Exegetical Commentary on the First Epistle of St. Paul to the Corinthians*. New York: Charles Scribner's Sons, 1916.

————. *Word Pictures in the New Testament*. 6 vols. Nashville, Tenn.: Broadman Press, 1930.

Ryrie, Charles Caldwell. *Biblical Theology of the New Testament*. Chicago: Moody Press, 1959.

Schaff, Philip. *History of the Christian Church*. 8 vols. Grand Rapids: Wm. B. Eerdmans Publishing Company, 1952.

Scofield, C. I. *Plain Papers on the Doctrine of the Holy Spirit*. New York: Fleming H. Revell Company, 1899.

Sherrill, John L. *They Speak With Other Tongues*. New York: McGraw-Hill Book Company, 1964.

Stegall, Carroll, Jr. *The Modern Tongues and Healing Movement*. Atlanta, Ga.: By the author, n.d.

Stolee, H. J. *Speaking in Tongues*. Minneapolis: Augsburg Publishing House, 1963.

Swete, Henry Barclay. *The Holy Spirit in the Ancient Church*. London: Macmillan and Co., 1912.

Tenney, Merrill C. *The Zondervan Pictorial Bible Dictionary*. Grand Rapids: Zondervan Publishing House, 1963.

Thayer, Joseph Henry. *A Greek-English Lexicon of the New Testament*. Edinburgh: T. & T. Clark, 1953.

The Englishman's Greek Concordance of the New Testament. London: Samuel Bagster and Sons, n.d.

Thomas, W. H. Griffith. *The Holy Spirit of God*. Chicago: The Bible Institute Colportage Ass'n, 1913.

Torrey, R. A. *The Baptism with the Holy Spirit.* New York: Fleming H. Revell Company, 1897.

Unger, Merrill F. *The Baptizing Work of the Holy Spirit.* Chicago: Scripture Press, 1953.

Vincent, Marvin R. *Word Studies in the New Testament.* 4 vols. New York: Charles Scribner's Sons, 1908.

Vine, W. E. *An Expository Dictionary of New Testament Words.* Westwood, N. J.: Fleming H. Revell Company, 1959.

Walvoord, John F. *The Holy Spirit.* Wheaton, Ill.: Van Kampen Press, 1954.

Wuest, Kenneth S. *Treasures from the Greek New Testament.* Grand Rapids: Wm. B. Eerdmans Publishing Co., 1942.

————. *Untranslatable Riches from the Greek New Testament.* Grand Rapids: Wm. B. Eerdmans Publishing Company, 1943.

Zodhiates, Spiros. *What the Bible Says About Tongues.* 6 booklets. Ridgefield, N. J.: American Mission to Greeks, Inc., 1964.

B. BOOKS: PARTS OF SERIES

Augustine. "On Baptism, Against the Donatists." Trans. J. R. King. Vol. IV of *The Nicene and Post-Nicene Fathers.* First Series. Ed. Philip Schaff. Buffalo: The Christian Literature Company, 1887.

————. "Ten Homilies on the First Epistle of John." Trans. H. Browne. Vol. VII of *The Nicene and Post-Nicene Fathers.* Ed. Philip Schaff. New York: The Christian Literature Company, 1888.

Chrysostom. "Homilies on First Corinthians." Trans. T. W. Chambers. Vol. XII of *The Nicene and Post-Nicene Fathers.* First Series. Ed. Philip Schaff. New York: The Christian Literature Company, 1889.

Eusebeius. "Church History." Trans. A. C. McGiffert. Vol. I of *The Nicene and Post-Nicene Fathers.* Second Series. Eds. Philip Schaff and Henry Wace. Grand Rapids: Wm. B. Eerdmans Publishing Company, 1961.

Findlay, G. G. "St. Paul's First Epistle to the Corinthians," *The Expositor's Greek New Testament.* Vol. II. Edited by W. Robertson Nicoll. Grand Rapids: Wm. B. Eerdmans Publishing Company, 1951.

Gerstner, John H. "Acts," *The Biblical Expositor.* Carl F. H. Henry (ed.). Vol. 3. Philadelphia: A. J. Holman Company, 1960.

Irenaeus. "Against Heresies." Vol. I of *The Ante-Nicene Fathers.* Eds. Alexander Roberts and James Donaldson. Grand Rapids: Wm. B. Eerdmans Publishing Company, 1950.

Justin Martyr. "Dialogue with Trypho." Vol. I of *The Ante-Nicene Fathers.* Eds. Alexander Roberts and James Donaldson. Grand Rapids: Wm. B. Eerdmans Publishing Company, 1950.

Knowling, R. J. "The Acts of the Apostles," *The Expositor's Greek Testament.* Vol. II. Edited by W. Robertson Nicoll. Grand Rapids: Wm. B. Eerdmans Publishing Company, 1951.

Origen. "Against Celsus." Trans. Frederick Crombie. Vol. IV of *The Ante-Nicene Fathers.* Eds. Alexander Roberts and James Donaldson. Grand Rapids: Wm. B. Eerdmans Publishing Company, 1951.

Plato. "Dialogues of Plato." Trans. Benjamin Jowett. Vol. VII of *Great Books of the Western World,* R. M. Hutchins (ed.). Chicago: Encyclopaedia Britannica, Inc., 1952.

————. "Ion," in the "Dialogues of Plato," Sec. 533-534. Trans. Benjamin Jowett. Vol. 7 of *Great Books of the Western World,* R. M. Hutchins (ed.). Chicago: Encyclopaedia Britannica, Inc., 1952.

————. "Phaedrus," in the "Dialogues of Plato," Sec. 244. Trans. Benjamin

Jowett. Vol. 7 of *Great Books of the Western World*, R. M. Hutchins (ed.). Chicago: Encyclopaedia Britannica, Inc., 1952.

———. "Timaeus," in the "Dialogues of Plato," Sec. 71-72. Trans. Benjamin Jowett. Vol. 7 of *Great Books of the Western World*, R. M. Hutchins (ed.). Chicago: Encyclopaedia Britannica, Inc., 1952.

Tertullian. "Against Marcion." Trans. Peter Holmes. Vol. III of *The Ante-Nicene Fathers*. Eds. Alexander Roberts and James Donaldson. Grand Rapids: Wm. B. Eerdmans Publishing Company, 1951.

Virgil. "Aeneid," Book VI. Trans. James Rhoades. Vol. XIII of *Great Books of the Western World*, R. M. Hutchins (ed.). Chicago: Encyclopaedia Britannica, Inc., 1952.

C. ARTICLES AND PERIODICALS

"Against Glossolalia," *Time*, LXXXI (May 17, 1963), 84.

Bach, Marcus. "Whether There Be 'Tongues'," *Christian Herald* (May, 1964), 10-11,20.

Barnhouse, Donald Grey. "Finding Fellowship with Pentecostals," *Eternity*, IX (April, 1958), 8-10.

Barth, Markus. "A Chapter on the Church — The Body of Christ," *Interpretation*, XII (April, 1958), 131-156.

Basham, Don W. "I Saw My Church Come to Life," *Christian Life*, XXVI (March, 1965), 37-39.

Beare, Frank W. "Speaking With Tongues," *Journal of Biblical Literature*, LXXXIII (September, 1964), 229-246.

Bellshaw, William G. "The Confusion of Tongues," *Bibliotheca Sacra*, CXX (April-June, 1963), 145-153.

Bennett, Dennis. "The Charismatic Renewal and Liturgy," *View* II (No. 1, 1965), 1-6.

Bergsma, Stuart. "Speaking With Tongues," *Torch and Trumpet*, XIV (November, 1964), 8-11.

———. "Speaking With Tongues," *Torch and Trumpet*, XIV (December, 1964), 9-13.

Bess, S. Herbert. "The Office of the Prophet in Old Testament Times," *Grace Journal*, I (Spring, 1960), 7-12.

"Blue Tongues," *Time*, LXXXI (March 29, 1963), 52.

Boer, Harry R. "The Spirit: Tongues and Message," *Christianty Today*, VII (January 4, 1963), 6-7).

Boyer, James L. "The Office of the Prophet in New Testament Times," *Grace Journal*, I (Spring, 1960), 13-20.

Brandt, Robert L. "Tongues . . . For a Sign," *The Pentecostal Evangel* (April 26, 1964), pp. 3-5.

Bredesen, Harold. "Discovery at Hillside," *Christian Life*, XX (January, 1959), 16-18.

———. "Return to the Charismata," *Trinity*, II (Whitsuntide, 1962), 22.

Callaghan, Michael. Letter to the Editor, *Time*, LXXVI (September, 5, 1960), p. 2.

Chinn, Jack J. "May We Pentecostals Speak," *Christianity Today*, V (July 17, 1961), 8-9.

Christenson, Larry. "Miracles are no Commonplace Here," *Christian Life*, XXVII (June, 1965), 36-37, 52-54.

Dirks, Lee E. "'Tongues' and the Historic Churches," *The National Observer*, October 26, 1964.

Dollar, George W. "Church History and the Tongues Movement," *Bibliotheca Sacra*, CXX (October-December, 1963), 316-321.

Edman, V. Raymond. "Divine or Devilish?" *Christian Herald* (May, 1964), 14-17.

————. Letter to the Editor, *Christianity Today*, VIII (October 25, 1963), 23.

Ewald, Tod W. "Aspects of Tongues," *View*, II (No. 1, 1965), 7-11.

Failing, George E. "Should I Speak with Tongues," *The Wesleyan Methodist*, CXXII (January 20, 1965), p. 6.

Farrell, Frank. "Outburst of Tongues: The New Penetration," *Christianity Today*, VII (September 13, 1963), 3-7.

"Fastest-Growing Church in the Hemisphere," *Time*, LXXX (November 2, 1962), p. 56.

Finch, John G. "God-Inspired or Self-Induced," *Christian Herald* (May, 1964), 12-13, 17-19.

Frame, Raymond. "Something Unusual," *His*, XXIV (December, 1963), 18-30.

"Francis Xavier," *The Catholic Encyclopedia*. Vol. VI. New York: The Encyclopedia Press, Inc., 1913.

Gaebelein, Arno C. "The So-Called Gift of Tongues," *Our Hope*, XIV (July, 1907), 13-16.

Gilmour, S. MacLean. "Easter and Pentecost," *Journal of Biblical Literature*, LXXXI (March, 1962), 62-66.

Harrison, Everett F. "The Holy Spirit in Acts and the Epistles," *Christianity Today*, I (May 27, 1957), 3ff.

Hayford, Jack. Letter to the Editor, *Christianity Today*, VIII (October 25, 1963), 22.

"Hildegard," *The Catholic Encyclopedia*. Vol. VII. New York: The Encyclopedia Press, Inc., 1913.

Hills, James W. L. "The New Pentecostalism: Its Pioneers and Promoters," *Eternity*, XIV (July, 1963), 17-18.

Hodges, Zane C. "The Purpose of Tongues," *Bibliotheca Sacra*, CXX (July-September, 1963), 226-233.

Hay, Albert L. "Flame in the Sanctuary," *The Pentecostal Herald* (April 26, 1964), pp. 14-15.

Hoyt, Herman A. "Speaking in Tongues," *Brethren Missionary Herald*, XXV, (March 23, 1963), 156-57.

————. "Speaking in Tongues," *Brethren Missionary Herald*, XXV (April 20, 1963), 204-07.

Hughes, Philip Edgcumbe. "Review of Christian Religious Thought," *Christianity Today*, VI (May 11, 1962), p. 63.

Hurst, D. V. "How to Receive the Baptism with the Holy Ghost," *The Pentecostal Evangel* (April 26, 1964), pp. 7-9.

Hurst, Wesley R., Jr. "Upon All Flesh," *The Pentecostal Evangel* (May 2, 1965), 11-12.

"Interesting Facts About the Assemblies of God," *The Pentecostal Evangel* (September 16, 1962), p. 12.

Johansson, Nils. "I Cor. XIII and I Cor. XIV," *New Testament Studies*, X (April, 1964), 383-392.

Johnson, S. Lewis, Jr. "The Gift of Tongues and the Book of Acts," *Bibliotheca Sacra*, CXX (October-December, 1963), 309-311.

Kooistra, Remkes. "I Would That Ye All Spake With Tongues," *Torch and Trumpet*, XIV (October, 1964), 8-10.

Mac Donald, William G. "Glossolalia in the New Testament," *Bulletin of the Evangelical Theological Society*, VII (Spring, 1964), 59-68.

Mahoney, Ralph. "Pentecost in Perspective," *Full Gospel Business Men's Voice*, XIII (May, 1965), 4-7.

May, F. William. "The Holy Spirit's Gift of Tongues," *Voice*, XLII (October, 1963), 4-5.

McCasland, S. Vernon. "Signs and Wonders," *Journal of Biblical Literature*, LXXVI (June, 1957), 149-152.

McCorkle, R. O. "Witness to the World," *Full Gospel Business Men's Voice*, XIII (February, 1965), 21-23, 28.

Miles, John. "Tongues," *Voice*, XLIV (February, 1965), 5-6.

————. "Basic Bible Approach and Interpretation," *Voice*, XLIV (March, 1965), 8-9.

————. "The Basic Nature of Gifts," *Voice*, XLIV, (April, 1965), 8-9.

————. "Spiritual Gifts and Christian Victory," *Voice*, XLIV (May, 1965), 8-9.

Moody, Dale. "Charismatic and Official Ministries," *Interpretation*, XIX (April, 1965), 168-181.

Morris, Leon. "Gifts of the Spirit's Free Bounty," *The Sunday School Times*, CVI (December 12, 1964), 5-7, 14-15.

Munn, G. Lacoste. "The Historical Background of First Corinthians," *Southwestern Journal of Theology*, III (October, 1960), 5-14.

Osteen, John H. "He Heard God Speak," *Baptists and the Baptism of the Holy Spirit* (Los Angeles: FGBMFI, 1963), 6-10.

Pierson, Arthur T. "Speaking With Tongues," *Our Hope*, XIV (July, 1907), 35-42.

Phillips, McCandlish. "'And There Appeared to Them Tongues of Fire'," *Saturday Evening Post* (May 16, 1964), 31-40.

Prange, Erwin. "A New Ministry," *Full Gospel Business Men's Voice*, XIII (April, 1964), 4-8, 18-26.

"Rector and a Rumpus," *Newsweek*, LVI (July 4, 1960), p. 77.

Reed, William Standish. "Family Doctor," *Christian Life*, XXVII (June, 1965), p. 24.

Rice, John R. "Should One Talk in Tongues to Edify Self?" *The Sword of the Lord*, (September 19, 1952).

Rice, Robert. "Charismatic Revival," *Christian Life*, XXV (November, 1963), 30-32.

————. "Charismatic Revival," *View*, II (No. 1, 1965), 12-16, 22.

Richardson, Richard A. "I Fought It, Then I Sought It," *Full Gospel Business Men's Voice*, XI (December, 1963), 18-20.

Rogers, Cleon L., Jr. "The Gift of Tongues in the Post Apostolic Church," *Bibliotheca Sacra*, CXXII (April-June, 1965), 134-143.

Schweiter, Edward. "The Service of Worship," *Interpretation*, XIII (October, 1959), 400-408.

Sirks, G. J. "The Cinderella of Theology: The Doctrine of the Holy Spirit," *Harvard Theological Review*, L (April, 1957), 77-80.

Smith, Kenneth G. "The 'Mystery' of the Holy Spirit," *Blue Banner Faith and Life*, XIX (January-March, 1964), 3-6.

Smith, Wilbur M. "Notes on the Literature of Pentecostalism," *Moody Monthly*, LVI (December, 1955, 33-37.

Soltan, George. "The Tongues Movement," *Our Hope*, LV (June, 1949), 751-55.

"Speaking in Tongues," *Time*, LXXVI (August 15, 1960), 53-55.

"Speaking With Other Tongues," *The Pentecostal Evangel* (April 26, 1964), pp. 9-11.

Stagg, Frank. "The Motif of First Corinthians," *Southwestern Journal of Theology*, III (October, 1960), 15-24.

Stiles, J. E., Jr. Letter to the Editor. *Christianity Today*, VIII (November 8, 1963), 17.

Stone, Jean. "What is Happening Today in the Episcopal Church?" *Christian Life*, XXIII (November, 1961), 38-41.

————. "Would You Like a Christian Advance?" *Trinity*, II (Christmastide, 1962-1963), 51.

Stonehouse, N. B. "Repentance, Baptism, and the Gift of the Holy Spirit," *The Westminster Theological Journal*, XIII (November, 1950), 1-18.

"Taming the Tongues," *Time*, LXXXIV (July 10, 1964), 65-66.

"The Holy Ghost," *Time,* LXXVI (September 12, 1960), 71.

"The Key to Spiritual Discovery," *The Pentecostal Evangel* (April 26, 1964), pp. 2-3.

"The Neo-Penecostal Movement," *The Pentecostal Evangel* (May 2, 1965), 2-5.

"The Third Force in Christendom." *Life,* XLIV (June 9, 1958), 113-124.

"This Church Found the God of Power," *Christian Life,* XXI (July, 1959), 14-15.

Topping, John. "Hearts Aflame," *Full Gospel Business Men's Voice,* XIII (February 1965), 3-7.

Toussaint, Stanley D. "First Corinthians Thirteen and the Tongues Question," *Bibliotheca Sacra,* CXX (October-December, 1963), 311-316.

"Traffic Hazard," *His,* XXIV (December, 1963), 42-45.

Unger,, Merrill F. "The Significance of Pentecost," *Bibliotheca Sacra,* CXXII (April-June, 1965), 169-177.

Van Elderen, Bastian. "Glossolalia in the New Testament," *Bulletin of the Evangelical Theological Society,* VII (Spring, 1964), 53-58.

"Vincent Ferrer," *The Catholic Encyclopedia.* Vol. XV. New York: The Encyclopedia Press, Inc., 1913.

Walker, Robert. "Church on the Mountaintop," *Christian Life,* XXV (July, 1963), 27-31.

Walters, Stanley D. "Speaking in Tongues," *Youth in Action* (May, 1964), 8-11, 28. Reprint.

Welmes, William. Letter to the Editor, *Christianity Today,* VIII (November 8, 1963), 19-20.

Zimmerman, Thomas F. "Plea for the Pentecostalists," *Christianity Today,* VII (January 4, 1963), 11-12.

———. "The Pentecostal Position," *The Pentecostal Evangel* (February 10, 1963), pp. 2-3, 7.

D. UNPUBLISHED MATERIALS

Boyer, James L. "An Exposition of 1 Corinthians." Unpublished classroom notes, Grace Theological Seminary, 1964.

Cruver, William H. "The Greater Gifts in 1 Corinthians 12:31." Unpublished critical monograph, Grace Theological Seminary, 1963.

Dowden, Milton L. "Why did Paul Rebaptize the Twelve Disciples in Acts 19:1-7." Unpublished critical monograph. Grace Theological Seminary, 1950.

Fink, Paul R. "The Phenomenon of Tongues as Presented in Scripture." Unpublished research paper, Dallas Theological Seminary, 1960.

Morr, Harold Francis. "These Signs Shall Follow Them That Believe." Unpublished critical monograph, Grace Theological Seminary, 1953.

Roger, Adam Henry. "Tongues as a Sign A Critical Investigation of 1 Corinthians 14:22." Unpublished critical monograph, Grace Theological Seminary, 1950.

Ruble, Richard Lee. "A Scriptural Evaluation of Tongues in Contemporary Theology." Unpublished Th.D. dissertation, Dallas Theological Seminary, 1964.

Tamkin, Warren E. " 'That Which Is Perfect' I Corinthians 13:10." Unpublished critical monograph, Grace Theological Seminary, 1949.

Weaver, Gilbert B. " 'Tongues Shall Cease': 1 Corinthians 13:8." Unpublished research paper, Grace Theological Seminary, 1964.

Zimmerman, Charles. "The Gift of Tongues in 1 Corinthians." Unpublished research paper, Grace Theological Seminary, n.d.

E. TRACTS AND REPRINTS

Bennett, Dennis J. *When Episcopalians Start Speaking in Tongues.* Medford, Oregon: Christian Retreat Center, n.d.

Bredesen, Harold. "Discovery at Yale." Reprint from Chrismastide 1962-63 issue of *Trinity* magazine. Van Nuys, Calif.: Blessed Trinity Society, 1963.

Christenson, Larry. *A Lutheran Pastor Speaks.* Van Nuys, California: The Blessed Trinity Society, n.d.

Haldeman, I. M. *Holy Ghost Baptism and Speaking with Tongues.*

Letter from an Anglican Priest to a Spiritual Child. Van Nuys, California: Blessed Trinity Society.

Ness, Henry H. *The Baptism with the Holy Spirit—What Is It?* Hayward, California: Evangelism Crusaders, Inc., n.d.

Return to the Charismata. Van Nuys, California: Blessed Trinity Society.

Stone, Jean. *What is Happening Today in the Episcopal Church?* Van Nuys, Calif.: The Blessed Trinity Society, n.d. Reprint from *Christian Life* (November, 1961).

————, and Bredesen, Harold. *The Charismatic Renewal in the Historic Churches.* Van Nuys, California: Blessed Trinity Society. Reprint from *Trinity* Magazine (Trinitytide, 1963).

What Next? Van Nuys, California: Blessed Trinity Society.

F. OTHER SOURCES

Assembly of God Church, Xenia, Ohio. Observations of the Sunday evening service and personal interview with pastor, Robert Dalton, author of *Tongues Like as of Fire.* May 16, 1965.

CBS Evening News, Walter Kronkite Reporting. Special report on speaking tongues featuring Harold Bredesen. April 21, 1965.

"Conversation Piece" radio program, Station WHIO, Dayton, Ohio. Questions and answers, featuring Billy Graham. November 16, 1964.

First Pentecostal Church, Xenia, Ohio. Attendance and observations at the Sunday evening service. May 30, 1965.

Full Gospel Business Men's Fellowship International Banquet, Dayton, Ohio. Personal observations of the procedures. May 21, 1965.

INDEX OF NAMES AND SUBJECTS